Paper Clips & Pet Rocks

Turning Your Idea into a Product That Sells

Tom Sotis

Paper Clips & Pet Rocks: Turning Your Idea into a Product that Sells

© 2024 Thomas Sotis. All rights reserved.

ISNB # 978-1-300-92770-9

Imprint: Lulu.com

To my lifelong friend

Al Labonte

Contents

Introduction: From Spark to Success: The Journey of an Idea 7

Chapter 1: Brainstorming and Concept Development 14

Chapter 2: Market Research: Identifying Your Niche 24

Chapter 3: Prototyping: Turning Ideas into Tangible Products 36

Chapter 4: Creating a Business Plan: Strategy and Structure 47

Chapter 5: Funding Your Idea: From Bootstrapping to Investors 59

Chapter 6: Branding and Positioning: Crafting Your Identity 74

Chapter 8: Production and Scaling: From Prototype to Mass Production 105

Chapter 9: Distribution Channels: Getting Your Product to Market 120

Chapter 10: Measuring Success and Iteration: Continuous Improvement 136

Conclusion: The Journey Ahead: Embracing Innovation and Growth 147

Appendix: 50 Simple Ideas that Made Huge Profits 158

Introduction: From Spark to Success: The Journey of an Idea

Every great invention, product, or innovation starts with something deceptively simple: an idea. Whether it's a lightbulb moment while you're in the shower or a persistent thought that keeps coming back to you as you go about your daily routine, ideas have the potential to change the world. They can shape industries, revolutionize how we live, work, and play, and even create entirely new markets. However, having an idea is only the first step. The real challenge is taking that idea and turning it into something tangible—something that not only exists but serves the needs of others, stands out in the marketplace, and achieves lasting success.

In this book, we're going to explore that transformative journey—from spark to success. While it's easy to get caught up in the romantic notion of the "eureka" moment, the reality is that taking an idea from concept to market is a process that involves many steps, trials, and moments of learning. It requires careful planning, persistence, and a deep understanding of the market you're aiming to enter.

For aspiring entrepreneurs and innovators, this process may seem daunting, but it doesn't have to be. With the right tools, strategies, and mindset, you can bring your ideas to life. Whether you've just stumbled upon a potentially groundbreaking solution to a problem or have been nurturing an idea for years, this book is designed to guide you through every step of the process. From brainstorming and refining your concept to launching your product into the world, we'll cover all the essential stages of the entrepreneurial journey.

The Power of Ideas

It all begins with an idea. Ideas are the seeds of innovation, and history is filled with examples of individuals who had the courage to act on their ideas, leading to incredible inventions and discoveries. Think about Thomas Edison and the invention of the lightbulb, or Steve Jobs and the creation of the iPhone. These world-changing innovations started as mere thoughts—thoughts that grew into something more through relentless effort, research, experimentation, and perseverance.

But not every idea needs to revolutionize the world in order to be successful. Many of the most successful products in the market today address specific, everyday needs. Take Post-it Notes, for example. A simple adhesive-backed piece of paper may not seem revolutionary, but it solved a common problem and became an indispensable tool in offices and homes around the globe. The same goes for Velcro, which took inspiration from nature's burrs to create a fastener used in clothing, shoes, and countless other applications.

What makes an idea powerful isn't necessarily its complexity or scale—it's the ability to recognize a problem or need and provide a solution that people find valuable. This is the foundation of every successful product: identifying a gap, a pain point, or an inefficiency, and offering a solution that makes life easier or better for others.

Turning the Idea into a Product

While it's exciting to come up with a new idea, the real work begins when you start to flesh it out. It's one thing to have a vague notion of a product in your mind, but quite another to develop it into a fully realized concept that can be tested, improved, and eventually sold to others.

This is where the concept of product development comes into play. Product development is the process of refining your idea into something practical, functional, and desirable. It involves asking important questions: Who is this product for? What problem does it solve? How will it work in real life? Does it already exist in some form, and if so, how can yours be better or different?

The transition from idea to product requires validation and iteration. It's not enough to simply believe that your idea is great—you need to prove that there's a market for it. This means testing your assumptions, gathering feedback, and being willing to make changes based on what you learn. Many entrepreneurs fall into the trap of falling in love with their initial idea, only to realize later that it doesn't resonate with their target audience. That's why it's crucial to remain flexible and open to feedback during the early stages of development.

In this book, we'll walk you through the process of turning your idea into a prototype, testing it with real users, and refining it based on their input. You'll learn how to balance your vision with the practical needs of your customers and how to avoid common pitfalls that can derail the product development process.

The Importance of Market Research

One of the key themes we'll explore throughout this book is the importance of market research. Bringing an idea to market isn't just about building something—it's about building the right thing. In order to do that, you need to understand your market, your competition, and your target audience. This involves conducting thorough research to identify trends, analyze competitors, and pinpoint the needs and preferences of your potential customers.

Market research is a powerful tool that can guide you in making informed decisions about your product. It helps you identify the most promising market opportunities, avoid costly mistakes, and position your product for success. Whether you're developing a physical product, a service, or a piece of software, market research allows you to get inside the minds of your customers and understand what they truly want.

We'll delve into how to conduct market research, from using online tools and surveys to talking directly to potential customers. By gathering insights from your target market, you can validate your idea, identify the most important features of your product, and create a strategy for positioning it in the marketplace.

Building a Brand

Every successful product has a brand that supports it. Whether you realize it or not, brands influence our decisions every day. Think about the products you use regularly—whether it's the coffee you drink, the shoes you wear, or the smartphone in your pocket. Chances are, you don't just use these products because they serve a function. You use them because you identify with the brand and the values it represents.

Building a brand goes far beyond designing a logo or choosing a catchy name. Your brand is the story you tell, the values you communicate, and the way your product makes people feel. A strong brand can differentiate your product in a crowded marketplace, build trust with your customers, and create a lasting emotional connection that goes beyond the utility of your product.

Throughout this book, we'll explore the art and science of branding, from defining your brand's mission and values to crafting a consistent message that resonates with your target audience. You'll learn how to position your brand for success, how to build brand loyalty, and how to leverage your brand to create a lasting competitive advantage.

The Role of Marketing

Once your product is ready, the next step is getting it into the hands of customers. This is where marketing comes in. Marketing is the bridge between your product and the people who need it. It's the process of generating awareness, building interest, and driving sales.

In today's digital world, marketing has become more complex and multi-faceted than ever before. There are countless channels and platforms through which you can reach your audience—from social media and email campaigns to search engine optimization (SEO) and influencer partnerships. The challenge is knowing which strategies will be most effective for your specific product and audience.

Throughout this book, we'll guide you through the essential elements of creating a marketing plan. You'll learn how to identify the right channels for your product, how to create compelling content that resonates with your audience, and how to measure the success of your marketing efforts. Whether you're working with a limited budget or have the resources to invest in a full-scale campaign, you'll find practical tips for promoting your product effectively.

Funding and Scaling Your Idea

Many aspiring entrepreneurs are held back by one major concern: funding. How do you get the financial resources needed to turn your idea into a product, build a brand, and launch it into the market?

The good news is that there are more funding options available today than ever before. From bootstrapping and crowdfunding to venture capital and angel investors, there are many ways to raise the capital you need to bring your idea to life. In this book, we'll explore different funding strategies, help you understand the pros and cons of each, and guide you through the process of pitching your idea to investors.

Beyond funding, scaling your product is another important consideration. Once you've launched, how do you grow your business and expand your reach? Whether you're planning to scale through manufacturing, partnerships, or entering new markets, we'll cover strategies for scaling effectively and sustainably.

Overcoming Obstacles

No entrepreneurial journey is without its challenges. Along the way, you'll face obstacles—some expected, and others that come out of nowhere. There will be times when your product doesn't perform as well as you hoped, when you struggle to secure funding, or when you encounter unforeseen technical challenges. The key to success is not avoiding obstacles, but learning how to navigate them and turn setbacks into opportunities for growth.

In this book, we'll share stories from entrepreneurs who have faced and overcome these obstacles. You'll learn how to maintain resilience, adapt to changing circumstances, and keep moving forward even when the path ahead seems uncertain.

The Entrepreneurial Mindset

At the heart of this journey from idea to market is the entrepreneurial mindset. This mindset is characterized by a willingness to take risks, a passion for solving problems, and a relentless drive to create something of value. It's the ability to stay curious, to learn from failure, and to keep pushing forward even when the odds seem stacked against you.

Throughout this book, we'll emphasize the importance of developing and maintaining this mindset. By adopting the entrepreneurial mindset, you'll not only increase your chances of success but also find greater fulfillment in the process of turning your ideas into reality.

As we embark on this journey together, remember that the path from idea to market is not linear. There will be detours, unexpected challenges, and moments of doubt. But with the right strategies, tools, and mindset, you can overcome these obstacles and bring your idea to life. Whether you're a first-time entrepreneur or a seasoned innovator, this book will serve as your roadmap, guiding you every step of the way from spark to success.

So, are you ready to take the first step? Let's get started.

Chapter 1: Brainstorming and Concept Development

Every product, invention, or innovation begins with a simple idea. But how do we take that spark of creativity and turn it into something real? The first step in the entrepreneurial journey is brainstorming and developing a concept—moving from raw inspiration to a refined, viable idea that has the potential to become a successful product in the marketplace. This chapter will guide you through the process of harnessing your creativity, developing ideas effectively, and ensuring your concept solves a real-world problem or fulfills a genuine need.

Brainstorming is more than just sitting down with a notepad and jotting down random thoughts; it's a disciplined approach to idea generation, one that encourages creativity while also providing structure. Concept development, on the other hand, is the process of refining your brainstormed ideas into a concrete product or service that addresses a specific problem or opportunity in the marketplace.

The Power of Creativity

Creativity is often viewed as something mystical, an innate talent that only a few people possess. But in reality, creativity is a skill that can be cultivated and strengthened over time. The first step to unlocking creativity is understanding that ideas don't appear out of thin air—they are the result of curiosity, observation, and a willingness to explore new perspectives.

In the context of entrepreneurship, creativity is about looking at the world around you and identifying opportunities for innovation. It's about asking questions like, "Why is this done this way?" or "How could this be improved?" and then allowing your mind to explore possible answers. The more you engage in this type of thinking, the more natural it will become to generate creative ideas.

However, creativity doesn't thrive in a vacuum. It often requires structure to flourish. When brainstorming, it's essential to create an environment that encourages free thinking while also guiding that thinking toward a specific goal. Let's explore how to structure your brainstorming sessions for maximum creativity and effectiveness.

Effective Brainstorming Techniques

Effective brainstorming is about generating a large quantity of ideas without immediate judgment or criticism. The goal is to get as many thoughts and concepts on the table as possible. Quantity leads to quality, as even seemingly silly ideas can spark brilliant insights when explored further.

Here are several brainstorming techniques you can use to generate and develop ideas:

Mind Mapping

Mind mapping is a visual brainstorming technique that helps you explore ideas by branching out from a central concept. Start by writing your core idea in the center of a page or whiteboard, then draw branches that represent related concepts or subtopics. From there, you can continue branching out, adding new ideas as they come to you.

For example, if your core idea is "portable energy," you might create branches for "solar power," "battery technology," "wireless charging," and "renewable energy sources." Each of these branches can then lead to further exploration, helping you uncover new directions or applications for your idea.

Mind mapping encourages nonlinear thinking and helps you see connections between ideas that you might not have noticed otherwise.

Brainwriting

For those who feel overwhelmed by group brainstorming or feel that their voice gets lost in the process, brainwriting is an excellent alternative. In brainwriting, each participant writes down three to five ideas on a piece of paper within a set time limit (usually five minutes). The paper is then passed to the next person, who builds on those ideas or adds new ones. This process continues for several rounds, resulting in a rich pool of ideas without the pressure of immediate feedback or discussion.

Brainwriting allows individuals to think quietly and deeply before sharing their thoughts with the group, leading to more thoughtful and diverse ideas. It's particularly useful in settings where quieter team members might struggle to contribute in traditional brainstorming sessions.

Reverse Brainstorming

Sometimes, the best way to come up with a solution is to think in reverse. In reverse brainstorming, you start by identifying a problem and then asking how you could cause or worsen that problem. For example, if you're developing a product to make online shopping easier, you might ask, "How can I make online shopping more difficult?"

By thinking about what would create a negative outcome, you can often uncover the key pain points that your product needs to address. Reverse brainstorming forces you to look at the problem from a different perspective, helping you identify potential challenges and obstacles early in the development process.

SCAMPER Technique

The SCAMPER technique is a structured approach to brainstorming that involves asking seven types of questions to help you generate new ideas. SCAMPER stands for:

- **Substitute**: What can be substituted or replaced to improve the idea?
- **Combine**: Can you combine two ideas, products, or processes to create something new?
- **Adapt**: How can you adapt an existing idea to fit a different purpose or market?
- **Modify**: Can you modify the idea to make it more effective or appealing?
- **Put to another use**: Is there another use for this idea that you haven't considered?
- **Eliminate**: What can you remove to simplify the idea or make it more efficient?
- **Reverse/Rearrange**: What happens if you reverse or rearrange the components of the idea?

By systematically asking these questions, you can explore different angles and possibilities for your idea, leading to unexpected insights and improvements.

Rapid Ideation

Rapid ideation is a fast-paced brainstorming method where you generate as many ideas as possible within a short time frame—usually five to ten minutes. The key to rapid ideation is to write down every idea that comes to mind, no matter how unrealistic or outlandish it may seem. The goal is to push your brain to think creatively under pressure, which can lead to surprising breakthroughs.

Once the time is up, you can go back and review the ideas, identifying which ones have potential and which ones might need further refinement. Rapid ideation is particularly useful when you're feeling stuck or when you need to jumpstart your creative thinking.

Evaluating Your Idea: Does It Solve a Real Problem?

After you've generated a variety of ideas through brainstorming, the next step is to evaluate those ideas to determine which ones have the most potential. One of the most important questions to ask during this stage is: **Does my idea solve a real problem?**

Many entrepreneurs fall into the trap of developing products or services based on what they think is a good idea, rather than what the market actually needs. A product may be innovative, but if it doesn't address a genuine problem or fulfill a specific need, it's unlikely to succeed in the marketplace.

Here are some key factors to consider when evaluating your ideas:

Identify the Problem or Pain Point

The best ideas are those that solve a clear problem or alleviate a pain point for a specific group of people. Ask yourself: What problem does this idea solve? Who experiences this problem, and how significant is it in their daily lives?

For example, consider the development of Uber. The founders identified a common pain point: people had difficulty hailing taxis, especially during peak hours. Uber addressed this problem by creating an app that allowed users to request rides from their smartphones, making transportation more convenient and accessible.

By focusing on a well-defined problem, Uber was able to create a product that offered a clear solution, leading to widespread adoption.

Validate the Problem with Real Users

Once you've identified a problem, it's crucial to validate it with real users. Conduct interviews, surveys, and focus groups with people who are likely to experience the problem you're trying to solve. Ask them about their pain points, how they currently address those problems, and what their ideal solution would look like.

This type of feedback is invaluable because it helps you understand whether the problem is significant enough for people to pay for a solution. It also gives you insights into what features or characteristics your product must have to meet user needs effectively.

For example, if you're developing a new type of kitchen gadget, interview home cooks and ask them about the challenges they face in the kitchen. Their responses may reveal opportunities for improvement or guide you toward features that would make your product more appealing.

Assess Market Demand

Even if your idea solves a problem, it's essential to assess whether there's sufficient demand for the solution. A niche problem may not have a large enough market to support the development of a new product. On the other hand, solving a widespread issue could lead to high demand and scalability.

To assess market demand, conduct market research to identify how many people experience the problem you're addressing and how much they'd be willing to pay for a solution. Look at existing products or services that attempt to solve similar problems and analyze their success. This will give you a sense of whether there's a viable market for your idea.

Competitive Landscape

As you evaluate your idea, it's important to understand the competitive landscape. Are there other products or services already solving the same problem? If so, how does your idea differentiate itself?

Having competitors isn't necessarily a bad thing—it can actually validate that there's a demand for the solution. However, it's crucial to identify what sets your idea apart. Whether it's a unique feature, a more affordable price point, or a superior user experience, your product needs to have a distinct competitive advantage to succeed in a crowded market.

Refining Your Idea into a Viable Concept

After evaluating your ideas, you should have a clearer sense of which ones hold the most potential. Now it's time to refine those ideas into a viable concept that can be developed into a product or service.

Here are the steps to refine your idea:

Define Your Target Audience

The more specific you can be about who your product is for, the more effective you'll be in developing and marketing it. Think about your ideal customer: What are their demographics (age, gender, income level, etc.)? What are their behaviors and preferences? What motivates them to make purchasing decisions?

By defining your target audience, you'll be able to tailor your product to meet their needs more effectively. This will also help guide your marketing efforts later on, ensuring that you're reaching the right people with the right message.

Focus on Core Features

It's easy to get carried away with adding features and functionalities during the concept development phase. However, the most successful products are often those that start with a simple, core set of features that solve the primary problem effectively.

Focus on the core features that your product needs to have in order to deliver value to your target audience. Additional features can be added later as you gather feedback and iterate on your product, but in the early stages, simplicity is key.

Develop a Value Proposition

Your value proposition is a clear statement of the benefits your product offers and why it's better than other solutions on the market. It's what sets your product apart and makes it compelling to potential customers.

To craft a strong value proposition, think about the specific value your product delivers. Does it save time? Improve efficiency? Make life easier? By clearly communicating the value your product provides, you'll be able to attract the right customers and differentiate yourself from competitors.

Create a Prototype

Once you've refined your idea into a viable concept, the next step is to create a prototype. A prototype is a rough version of your product that allows you to test its functionality and gather feedback from potential users.

Creating a prototype doesn't have to be expensive or time-consuming. In fact, the goal of a prototype is to create a simple, low-cost version of your product that you can test and iterate on. We'll explore the process of prototyping in more detail in the next chapter, but for now, focus on refining your concept to the point where you can build a functional version of it.

Conclusion

Brainstorming and concept development are the foundational steps of the entrepreneurial journey. By harnessing your creativity, using effective brainstorming techniques, and evaluating your ideas through the lens of real-world problems, you can transform raw inspiration into a viable concept with the potential for market success.

Remember that the process of refining your idea is iterative. You'll need to be open to feedback, willing to make changes, and constantly testing your assumptions. But by taking a disciplined approach to brainstorming and concept development, you'll be well on your way to creating a product that serves the needs of others and stands out in the marketplace.

In the next chapter, we'll dive into the process of creating a prototype and testing your concept with real users, turning your idea into a tangible product that can be further refined and developed.

Chapter 2: Market Research: Identifying Your Niche

Market research is one of the most critical steps in taking an idea and turning it into a viable product. It involves systematically gathering and analyzing information about your target audience, competitors, and market conditions to help you make informed decisions. No matter how brilliant your idea is, if it doesn't fit the needs of the market or lacks competitive positioning, it is unlikely to succeed. In this chapter, we'll focus on how to conduct thorough market research to find where your idea fits, how to define your market, identify gaps, analyze trends, and understand your customers' needs. Additionally, we will cover competitive analysis to ensure your idea stands out in a crowded market.

The main goal of market research is to reduce the uncertainty involved in launching a product. By understanding your niche, target audience, and competitive landscape, you increase your chances of successfully bringing your product to market. With proper research, you can anticipate market demand, identify potential challenges, and refine your product to meet the needs of your customers.

The Importance of Market Research

Market research is essential because it allows you to validate your idea before investing time and money into development and marketing. It helps answer critical questions such as:

- Is there a demand for your product?
- Who are your target customers, and what are their needs?

- What problems does your product solve, and how are they currently being addressed?
- How many potential customers are there, and how much are they willing to pay?
- Who are your competitors, and how is your product different or better?

Without market research, you risk launching a product that no one wants, misjudging customer needs, or entering an oversaturated market without a clear competitive advantage. Market research enables you to gather data that can help you make strategic decisions about product development, pricing, marketing, and distribution.

Defining Your Market

The first step in market research is to define your market. This involves determining the overall market size, growth potential, and identifying the segment in which your product will operate. Start by asking, "What industry or market does my product fit into?" and "Who are my customers?"

When defining your market, you'll need to focus on the following key elements:

Total Addressable Market (TAM)

Your total addressable market (TAM) refers to the total revenue opportunity available if your product were to reach 100% of the market. It represents the maximum market size for your product and gives you a sense of how large the opportunity is. While it's unlikely that you'll capture the entire market, understanding the TAM helps you assess the potential for growth.

For example, if you're developing a new app for fitness enthusiasts, your TAM would include all potential users who are interested in fitness apps, wearable fitness technology, or digital fitness solutions. Understanding the size of this market will help you determine whether it's worth pursuing and what share of the market you might realistically capture.

Served Available Market (SAM)

Your served available market (SAM) is the portion of the TAM that your product can realistically serve based on factors like geography, product features, and distribution. SAM focuses on the specific segment of the market that is within your reach. For instance, if your fitness app is designed for English-speaking users, your SAM would exclude non-English-speaking markets, narrowing the potential customer base.

Target Market (TM)

Finally, your target market (TM) is the segment of customers that you'll actively pursue. This group represents the individuals or businesses that are most likely to buy your product. They share common characteristics such as demographics, behavior, and needs, and they are the people you'll focus on when creating your marketing strategy.

Your target market is crucial because it will guide all of your product development and marketing efforts. To define your target market, you'll need to conduct further research on customer demographics, psychographics (attitudes, values, and lifestyle), and behavior.

Identifying Gaps in the Market

Once you've defined your market, the next step is to identify gaps or unmet needs. Market gaps are opportunities where existing products are falling short or where demand exceeds supply. Finding these gaps can help you position your product in a way that meets the needs of underserved customers or solves problems that competitors are failing to address.

Customer Pain Points

One of the most effective ways to identify market gaps is to focus on customer pain points. Pain points are problems or frustrations that customers face with existing solutions. By addressing these pain points, you can create a product that provides a better experience than what's currently available.

To identify pain points, conduct customer surveys, interviews, and focus groups. Ask potential customers about their experiences with existing products in your market. What do they like or dislike? What features are they missing? What problems do they encounter when using these products?

For example, when Airbnb entered the market, they identified a gap in the hospitality industry. Traditional hotels often lacked the personal touch that travelers wanted, and there was a growing desire for more unique, affordable, and flexible accommodations. By addressing this pain point, Airbnb created a platform that allowed travelers to book short-term stays in people's homes, filling a gap in the market.

Competitive Analysis

Another way to identify market gaps is through competitive analysis. By studying your competitors, you can identify areas where their products fall short or where they fail to meet customer needs. This analysis will help you find opportunities to differentiate your product.

Start by identifying your direct and indirect competitors. Direct competitors offer similar products or services, while indirect competitors offer alternatives that solve the same problem in a different way. For example, if you're developing a meal delivery service, your direct competitors would be other meal delivery companies, while your indirect competitors might include grocery delivery services or restaurants offering takeout.

Once you've identified your competitors, analyze their strengths and weaknesses. Pay attention to the following factors:

- **Product features**: What features do their products offer, and how do they compare to your idea?

- **Pricing**: How do competitors price their products, and where could your product offer more value or better pricing?

- **Customer reviews**: Read customer reviews and feedback on competitor products. This can provide valuable insights into what customers like and dislike, and where there may be opportunities to improve.

- **Market positioning**: How are competitors positioning their products in the market? Are they targeting a different audience or addressing a different need than you?

By analyzing your competitors, you can identify gaps that your product can fill. For example, you may discover that most competitors in your market offer expensive, high-end solutions, leaving an opportunity for a more affordable, accessible product. Or you may find that competitors' products lack certain features that customers are demanding, giving you a chance to create a superior offering.

Emerging Trends

Keeping an eye on emerging trends in your market is another way to identify gaps and opportunities. Trends can reveal shifts in customer behavior, technology, or industry practices that create new needs or open up new markets. By staying ahead of these trends, you can position your product to take advantage of growing demand.

For example, the rise of remote work has created new opportunities for products and services that cater to home office setups, virtual collaboration tools, and flexible work arrangements. Entrepreneurs who recognized this trend early were able to create products that filled emerging needs in the remote work market.

To identify emerging trends, follow industry publications, attend conferences, and network with others in your field. Pay attention to changes in consumer behavior, technological advancements, and regulatory shifts that could impact your market.

Understanding Customer Needs

At the core of market research is understanding your customers. After all, your product's success depends on whether it meets the needs and expectations of the people who will be using it. Understanding customer needs involves more than just knowing their demographics—it requires deep insight into their behavior, motivations, preferences, and pain points.

Customer Segmentation

Customer segmentation is the process of dividing your target market into distinct groups based on shared characteristics. By segmenting your market, you can tailor your product and marketing efforts to meet the specific needs of each group.

There are several ways to segment your market:

- **Demographic segmentation**: This includes factors such as age, gender, income, education level, and occupation. For example, a luxury skincare brand may target affluent women in their 30s and 40s.

- **Psychographic segmentation**: This includes lifestyle, values, interests, and attitudes. For instance, a company selling eco-friendly products may target environmentally conscious consumers who prioritize sustainability.

- **Behavioral segmentation**: This focuses on how customers behave, such as their purchasing habits, brand loyalty, and product usage. A streaming service, for example, may target heavy users who frequently binge-watch TV shows.

By segmenting your market, you can create a more targeted and personalized product that resonates with specific customer groups. You can also develop marketing campaigns that speak directly to the needs and desires of each segment, increasing the likelihood of success.

Customer Personas

To gain a deeper understanding of your customers, it's helpful to create customer personas. A customer persona is a fictional representation of your ideal customer, based on research and data. Personas help you humanize your target audience and think about their needs, behaviors, and motivations on a more personal level.

When creating customer personas, include details such as:

- Name, age, gender, and occupation
- Lifestyle and hobbies
- Pain points and challenges
- Goals and motivations
- Buying behavior and decision-making process

For example, if you're developing a fitness app, one of your personas might be "Sarah, a 35-year-old working mother who wants to stay fit but struggles to find time for the gym." By understanding Sarah's challenges and motivations, you can design a product that fits her busy lifestyle, offering short, effective workouts that she can do at home.

Customer personas help guide product development by keeping the needs of your target audience front and center. They also provide valuable insights for marketing, as you can create messaging and content that speaks directly to the pain points and goals of each persona.

Gathering Customer Feedback

To truly understand your customers' needs, you need to gather direct feedback from them. This can be done through a variety of methods, including:

- **Surveys**: Online surveys allow you to collect quantitative data from a large number of respondents. You can ask questions about customer preferences, pain points, and purchasing behavior.

- **Interviews**: One-on-one interviews provide qualitative insights into your customers' experiences and motivations. Interviews allow you to ask open-ended questions and dive deeper into specific topics.

- **Focus groups**: In a focus group, you gather a small group of potential customers to discuss their thoughts on a product or idea. Focus groups provide real-time feedback and the opportunity to observe group dynamics.

- **Usability testing**: If you have a prototype or early version of your product, usability testing allows you to observe how customers interact with it. This helps you identify pain points and areas for improvement.

By gathering customer feedback, you can validate your assumptions, refine your product, and ensure that it meets the needs of your target audience. Feedback is especially valuable during the concept development phase, as it allows you to make adjustments before investing in full-scale production or marketing.

Competitive Analysis: Standing Out in a Crowded Market

Understanding your competitors is just as important as understanding your customers. In today's competitive landscape, few markets are completely untapped, which means you'll likely face competition from other products or services. To succeed, you need to differentiate your product and carve out a unique position in the market.

Identifying Competitors

The first step in competitive analysis is identifying your competitors. As mentioned earlier, competitors can be divided into two categories:

- **Direct competitors**: These are companies that offer products or services that are similar to yours and target the same audience. For example, if you're launching a new brand of organic snacks, your direct competitors would be other companies selling organic snacks.

- **Indirect competitors**: These are companies that offer different products but serve the same customer need. For example, a meal delivery service might face indirect competition from grocery delivery services, as both address the need for convenient meal solutions.

Identifying both direct and indirect competitors will give you a comprehensive view of the competitive landscape and help you spot opportunities for differentiation.

Analyzing Competitors

Once you've identified your competitors, analyze their products, marketing strategies, and customer base. This will help you understand what they're doing well and where there may be gaps or weaknesses that you can exploit.

Key factors to analyze include:

- **Product features**: Compare your product's features to those of your competitors. What makes your product unique? What features do competitors offer that you don't, and vice versa?

- **Pricing**: Analyze competitors' pricing strategies. Are they positioned as premium or budget options? How does your pricing compare, and what value do you offer in relation to the price?

- **Marketing**: Study competitors' marketing tactics, including their branding, messaging, and promotional strategies. How do they position themselves in the market, and what channels do they use to reach their audience?

- **Customer reviews**: Read reviews and testimonials for competitors' products. This will give you insights into what customers like and dislike, and where there may be opportunities to improve or differentiate your product.

Differentiating Your Product

After analyzing your competitors, the next step is to differentiate your product. Differentiation is the process of making your product stand out by offering something unique or better than what's currently available. This could be in the form of:

- **Product innovation**: Offering a new feature or functionality that competitors don't have.

- **Better pricing**: Providing a more affordable solution without compromising on quality.

- **Superior customer experience**: Offering exceptional customer service, faster delivery, or a more user-friendly interface.

- **Niche focus**: Targeting a specific niche or underserved segment of the market that competitors are overlooking.

The key to successful differentiation is to focus on what makes your product special and to communicate that value clearly to your target audience. This will help you carve out a unique position in the market and attract customers who resonate with your product's distinct advantages.

Conclusion

Market research is the foundation upon which successful products are built. By thoroughly understanding your target market, identifying gaps, and analyzing competitors, you can position your product for success and reduce the risks associated with launching a new idea. From defining your target audience to identifying emerging trends and differentiating your product, market research provides the insights needed to make informed decisions and stand out in a crowded market.

In the next chapter, we'll explore the process of prototyping and turning your idea into a tangible product that can be tested and refined based on real-world feedback.

Chapter 3: Prototyping: Turning Ideas into Tangible Products

Ideas are powerful, but their true value lies in their transformation from abstract thoughts into tangible, usable products. This transformation is where prototyping comes into play. A prototype is the first physical or digital representation of your idea—a working model that allows you to test your concept, gather feedback, and refine your product before moving to full-scale production. This chapter will explore the process of creating prototypes, covering various methods from low-cost mockups to high-fidelity models. We'll also discuss how to test your prototypes with real users to collect valuable feedback and improve your product design.

Creating a prototype is an essential step in product development, as it allows you to move beyond theory and get hands-on with your idea. A well-executed prototype can uncover unforeseen challenges, reveal new opportunities for improvement, and help you communicate your vision more effectively to stakeholders, investors, and customers.

Why Prototyping Is Critical

Prototyping is a fundamental step for several reasons. It provides a clear direction for the next stages of product development, ensures that your concept is feasible, and helps you avoid costly mistakes down the line. Here are some key benefits of prototyping:

Validation of Your Idea

A prototype brings your idea to life, allowing you to test its functionality, design, and usability. While your idea may seem perfect on paper, a prototype helps validate whether it works in practice. By interacting with a tangible version of your product, you can identify strengths, weaknesses, and areas that need improvement.

Early Detection of Flaws

Even the most carefully planned ideas can have hidden flaws. Prototypes help you identify potential issues early in the development process, whether they are related to design, materials, usability, or performance. By catching these problems before moving to full-scale production, you save time, money, and resources.

Gathering Feedback from Real Users

Prototyping allows you to test your product with real users and gather their feedback. This feedback is invaluable because it helps you understand how your target audience interacts with your product, what they like or dislike, and what improvements they'd like to see. Testing your prototype with users ensures that you're developing a product that truly meets their needs.

Refining Your Product Design

Prototypes provide a hands-on way to refine and iterate your product design. Based on user feedback and your own observations, you can make changes to improve functionality, usability, and aesthetics. Prototyping is an iterative process, and each version of your prototype should bring you closer to the final product.

Communicating Your Vision

Whether you're pitching your idea to investors, potential partners, or team members, a prototype can be a powerful communication tool. It's much easier to explain and showcase your product when you have a physical or digital model to demonstrate. A prototype makes your idea more tangible and helps others understand your vision more clearly.

Types of Prototypes

Prototypes can vary greatly in complexity, depending on the stage of development and the specific goals of the prototype. There are several types of prototypes, ranging from simple, low-cost mockups to fully functional models. Let's explore the different types of prototypes and when each is most appropriate.

Low-Fidelity Prototypes

Low-fidelity prototypes are rough, early-stage representations of your product. They are typically made from inexpensive materials or created using simple digital tools. The goal of a low-fidelity prototype is to quickly visualize your idea and test basic functionality or design concepts.

Examples of low-fidelity prototypes:

- **Sketches**: Hand-drawn sketches or diagrams that represent the product's layout or design. Sketches are an easy and fast way to communicate ideas and make initial design decisions.

- **Paper prototypes**: These are physical models made from paper, cardboard, or other inexpensive materials. Paper prototypes are commonly used for designing user interfaces or testing product dimensions and layout.
- **Wireframes**: In digital product development, wireframes are low-fidelity prototypes that outline the basic structure and layout of a website or app. They focus on functionality and navigation without worrying about design aesthetics.

Low-fidelity prototypes are useful for brainstorming, early-stage testing, and quickly iterating on ideas. They are not intended to represent the final product but are instead a tool for exploring and refining concepts.

Mid-Fidelity Prototypes

Mid-fidelity prototypes provide a more detailed representation of your product but are still not fully functional. These prototypes offer a higher level of detail than low-fidelity models and may include more accurate dimensions, materials, and components. Mid-fidelity prototypes are often used to test specific features or aspects of a product.

Examples of mid-fidelity prototypes:

- **3D-printed models**: If you're developing a physical product, 3D printing is a cost-effective way to create a prototype with accurate dimensions and a realistic appearance. 3D-printed prototypes allow you to test the product's size, shape, and ergonomics.
- **Digital mockups**: For software or digital products, a mid-fidelity prototype might include a more polished

user interface with basic interactive elements. Digital mockups help test usability and user experience before building the full product.

Mid-fidelity prototypes are ideal for testing more specific aspects of your product, such as its usability, ergonomics, or visual design. They provide a more realistic representation of your product, making them suitable for gathering user feedback.

High-Fidelity Prototypes

High-fidelity prototypes are fully functional models that closely resemble the final product in terms of design, materials, and functionality. These prototypes are often used for final testing, demonstrations, and presentations to stakeholders or investors.

Examples of high-fidelity prototypes:

- **Functional product models**: For physical products, a high-fidelity prototype would include the same materials and components as the final product. It should be fully operational, allowing you to test its performance and durability.

- **Interactive digital prototypes**: In the case of software, a high-fidelity prototype would be a fully interactive version of the app or website, complete with polished design elements and working features.

High-fidelity prototypes are the closest representation of the final product and are often used to validate that the product is ready for production. They are also used in marketing materials, product demonstrations, and investor pitches.

The Prototyping Process

Prototyping is an iterative process that involves multiple stages of development, testing, and refinement. The goal is to start with a basic representation of your idea and gradually improve it through feedback and iteration. Here's a step-by-step guide to the prototyping process:

Step 1: Define the Goals of Your Prototype

Before you begin creating a prototype, it's important to define the specific goals you want to achieve. Prototypes can serve different purposes depending on where you are in the product development process. Ask yourself:

- **What am I trying to learn or test?** Are you testing the product's functionality, design, or usability? Or are you validating whether your concept solves a real problem?

- **Who will use the prototype?** Will you be testing it with real users, presenting it to investors, or using it to make internal design decisions?

- **What level of fidelity do I need?** Depending on your goals, you may need a low-fidelity, mid-fidelity, or high-fidelity prototype. For early-stage testing, a low-fidelity prototype may be sufficient, while later stages may require a more detailed model.

By defining the goals of your prototype, you can determine the appropriate level of detail, materials, and functionality needed.

Step 2: Create a Low-Fidelity Prototype

The next step is to create a low-fidelity prototype. This is a rough, early-stage model that allows you to explore your idea and make initial design decisions. The goal of a low-fidelity prototype is to test basic concepts, such as the product's layout, dimensions, or key features.

For physical products, a low-fidelity prototype might be made from materials like paper, cardboard, or foam. For digital products, you might create wireframes or simple digital mockups. At this stage, don't worry about aesthetics or fine details—focus on testing the core functionality or structure of your idea.

Step 3: Test and Gather Feedback

Once you have a low-fidelity prototype, it's time to test it with real users and gather feedback. Testing doesn't have to be formal or expensive. You can start by showing your prototype to friends, colleagues, or potential customers to get their initial impressions. Ask questions like:

- **What do you like or dislike about the prototype?**
- **Does the prototype solve the problem it's intended to address?**
- **Is the product easy to use?**
- **What features would you like to see added or changed?**

At this stage, feedback is essential for identifying any major flaws or areas for improvement. Low-fidelity prototypes are easy and inexpensive to change, so don't be afraid to iterate based on the feedback you receive.

Step 4: Create a Mid-Fidelity Prototype

After refining your concept based on feedback, the next step is to create a mid-fidelity prototype. This version should be more detailed and accurate than the low-fidelity prototype, and it should include more realistic materials or digital elements.

For physical products, a mid-fidelity prototype might involve 3D printing or using materials that closely resemble the final product. For digital products, you might create a more polished user interface with interactive elements.

The goal of the mid-fidelity prototype is to test more specific aspects of your product, such as its ergonomics, usability, or design. At this stage, you should focus on refining the product's functionality and ensuring that it meets the needs of your target audience.

Step 5: Test Again and Iterate

As with the low-fidelity prototype, you'll need to test the mid-fidelity version with real users and gather feedback. This feedback will help you make further improvements and refine the product's design.

At this stage, testing should be more formal and structured. Consider conducting usability tests, where users interact with the prototype in a controlled environment while you observe their behavior. This will help you identify any usability issues or design flaws that need to be addressed.

Step 6: Create a High-Fidelity Prototype

Once you've refined your product through multiple rounds of testing and iteration, it's time to create a high-fidelity prototype. This version should be as close to the final product as possible, both in terms of design and functionality.

For physical products, this might involve using the same materials and manufacturing processes that will be used in production. For digital products, a high-fidelity prototype should include fully interactive features, polished design elements, and smooth functionality.

High-fidelity prototypes are typically used for final testing, presentations, and demonstrations. They allow you to validate that your product is ready for production and provide a clear representation of what the final product will look like.

Step 7: Test and Validate

The final step in the prototyping process is to test the high-fidelity prototype and validate that it meets all of your goals. This is your last opportunity to gather feedback and make any necessary adjustments before moving to production.

At this stage, testing should be as close to real-world conditions as possible. For physical products, this might involve stress testing, durability testing, or performance testing. For digital products, it might involve testing on different devices or platforms to ensure compatibility and performance.

Once you've validated that the high-fidelity prototype is functional, user-friendly, and ready for production, you can move on to the next phase of product development.

Testing Prototypes with Real Users

One of the most valuable aspects of prototyping is the ability to test your product with real users and gather feedback. User testing provides insights into how people interact with your product, what challenges they encounter, and what improvements they would like to see.

Here are some best practices for testing prototypes with real users:

Recruit the Right Participants

The participants you choose for user testing should closely resemble your target audience. If your product is designed for a specific demographic or user group, make sure that the participants match those characteristics. The more closely aligned the participants are with your target market, the more valuable the feedback will be.

Set Clear Objectives

Before conducting user testing, define the specific objectives you want to achieve. Are you testing usability, functionality, or design? Do you want to see how users interact with a specific feature? By setting clear objectives, you can ensure that the testing session provides actionable insights.

Observe and Ask Open-Ended Questions

During user testing, observe how participants interact with the prototype. Take note of any difficulties they encounter, as well as their overall experience. Ask open-ended questions to encourage participants to share their thoughts and opinions. For example:

- **What do you think of the product's design?**
- **How easy or difficult was it to complete this task?**
- **What improvements would you suggest?**

Open-ended questions encourage participants to provide detailed feedback, which can help you identify areas for improvement.

Iterate Based on Feedback

User testing is an iterative process. After gathering feedback, use it to make improvements to your prototype. Continue testing and iterating until you've addressed all major issues and are confident that the product meets the needs of your target audience.

Conclusion

Prototyping is a crucial step in transforming your idea into a tangible, functional product. By creating prototypes, testing them with real users, and iterating based on feedback, you can refine your concept, address potential issues, and ensure that your product is ready for production. Whether you're developing a physical product or a digital solution, the prototyping process allows you to validate your ideas, make informed design decisions, and ultimately create a product that meets the needs of your customers.

In the next chapter, we'll explore how to create a comprehensive business plan to guide your product's development and launch, from setting goals to securing funding and building a roadmap for growth.

Chapter 4: Creating a Business Plan: Strategy and Structure

Turning an idea into a tangible product is an exciting step in the entrepreneurial journey, but to bring your concept to market successfully, you need more than just a prototype. You need a clear strategy and a well-structured roadmap for execution. This is where the business plan comes into play. A business plan is your blueprint for launching and growing your product in the marketplace. It outlines your goals, defines your strategy, and sets the foundation for how you'll operate, market, and scale your business.

Creating a comprehensive business plan is crucial for several reasons. It helps you clarify your vision, identify potential challenges, and ensure that your product is aligned with market demand. Moreover, a solid business plan is often required when seeking investment, partnerships, or loans. Investors and partners want to see that you have a clear plan for generating revenue, managing expenses, and growing the business.

In this chapter, we'll guide you through the process of writing a detailed business plan, including setting goals, financial projections, marketing strategies, and creating a roadmap for growth. Whether you're seeking investors, partners, or simply want to ensure your business is set up for success, a well-structured business plan will provide the direction you need.

Why a Business Plan is Critical

A business plan is not just a document for external stakeholders; it's an essential tool for you as an entrepreneur.

It forces you to think critically about every aspect of your business, from operations to finances, and helps you identify risks and opportunities before they arise.

Here are some key reasons why a business plan is essential:

Clarifying Your Vision

Having a great idea is one thing, but turning that idea into a viable business requires clarity and focus. A business plan helps you clearly define what your product is, who it's for, and how it fits into the market. It forces you to articulate your goals, strategy, and long-term vision, ensuring that every aspect of your business is aligned with your overall mission.

Guiding Your Growth Strategy

A business plan provides a roadmap for growth, helping you set milestones and track your progress. It lays out the steps you need to take to reach your goals, from product development to marketing and sales. Without a business plan, it's easy to get lost in day-to-day operations without making meaningful progress toward your long-term objectives.

Securing Investment

If you're seeking investment or funding, a business plan is often a requirement. Investors want to see that you have a clear strategy for generating revenue and achieving profitability. They'll also look for detailed financial projections, market research, and a clear understanding of the competitive landscape. A well-written business plan demonstrates that you've done your homework and are prepared to execute your vision.

Managing Risk

Starting a business is inherently risky, but a well-structured business plan helps you anticipate challenges and develop strategies for mitigating risk. By thinking through potential obstacles in advance, you can prepare for them and minimize their impact on your business.

Aligning Your Team

As your business grows, you'll likely bring on team members, partners, or advisors. A business plan helps align everyone around a common vision and set of goals. It provides a shared understanding of where the business is headed and how you plan to get there.

Key Components of a Business Plan

A business plan typically consists of several key sections, each serving a specific purpose. While the exact structure of your business plan may vary depending on your industry and audience, the following components are essential for creating a comprehensive plan:

1. **Executive Summary**
2. **Company Overview**
3. **Market Research and Analysis**
4. **Product or Service Description**
5. **Marketing and Sales Strategy**
6. **Operations Plan**
7. **Financial Plan**

8. **Appendix**

Let's dive into each of these sections in detail.

Executive Summary

The executive summary is the first section of your business plan, but it's often written last. It provides a concise overview of your entire business plan, summarizing key points from each section. The goal of the executive summary is to capture the reader's attention and provide a high-level snapshot of your business.

The executive summary should include:

- **Business Overview**: A brief description of your product, the problem it solves, and your target market.

- **Mission Statement**: A clear, concise statement of your business's mission and purpose.

- **Goals**: Key objectives you aim to achieve, such as launching your product, reaching specific revenue targets, or expanding into new markets.

- **Value Proposition**: A summary of what sets your product apart from competitors and why customers will choose it.

- **Financial Highlights**: An overview of your financial projections, including revenue goals, profit margins, and funding requirements.

- **Call to Action**: If you're seeking investment or partnerships, clearly state what you're looking for and how the reader can get involved.

The executive summary should be no longer than one or two pages. Remember, this is the first impression investors or partners will have of your business, so make sure it's compelling and concise.

Company Overview

The company overview provides more detail about your business and its structure. It explains who you are, what your business does, and what makes it unique. The company overview should include:

- **Company Name**: The official name of your business.

- **Legal Structure**: Whether your business is a sole proprietorship, partnership, corporation, or LLC.

- **Location**: Where your business is based and whether you operate locally, nationally, or globally.

- **Mission and Vision**: Your long-term vision for the company and the mission that drives your work.

- **Business History**: If your business is already operational, provide a brief history of its founding and key milestones.

- **Team**: An introduction to your key team members, their roles, and relevant experience. This section is particularly important if you're seeking investment, as investors often place significant value on the strength of the founding team.

The company overview should give readers a clear sense of who you are, what you do, and why you're well-positioned to succeed.

Market Research and Analysis

In this section, you'll present the market research that validates the demand for your product and outlines your target audience. The goal is to demonstrate that there is a real need for your product and that you understand your market and competition.

Here's what to include:

- **Market Overview**: A high-level view of your industry and its growth potential. Include data on market size, trends, and key drivers of demand.

- **Target Market**: Define your target market by breaking it down into specific segments. Include details on demographics (age, gender, income, location) and psychographics (lifestyle, values, purchasing behavior).

- **Customer Needs and Pain Points**: Describe the key problems or needs your target market faces and how your product addresses them.

- **Competitive Analysis**: Identify your main competitors and analyze their strengths and weaknesses. Explain how your product is different and what gives you a competitive advantage.

- **Market Positioning**: Define how you plan to position your product within the market. Are you targeting a premium segment, offering a more affordable alternative, or filling a specific niche?

Market research is crucial for convincing investors and partners that there is a viable opportunity for your product. Be sure to back up your claims with data and evidence.

Product or Service Description

This section is where you provide a detailed description of your product or service. You'll explain what your product does, how it works, and what makes it unique. Key elements to include are:

- **Product Features**: A breakdown of the key features and functionalities of your product.

- **Unique Selling Proposition (USP)**: What sets your product apart from competitors? Why will customers choose your product over others?

- **Development Stage**: If your product is still in development, outline the current stage and the next steps in the process.

- **Intellectual Property**: If you have patents, trademarks, or other forms of intellectual property, mention them here.

- **Customer Benefits**: Focus on how your product benefits the customer. What problem does it solve? How does it improve the customer's life or business?

If you have a working prototype or early version of your product, this is the section where you describe it in detail. Use visuals, such as images or diagrams, if necessary to help readers understand the product's design and functionality.

Marketing and Sales Strategy

A great product is only valuable if people know about it. In this section, you'll outline your strategy for reaching your target market and driving sales. Here's what to cover:

- **Marketing Goals**: What are your marketing objectives? For example, do you want to generate brand awareness, drive online sales, or enter a new geographic market?

- **Pricing Strategy**: How do you plan to price your product? Will you use a premium pricing model, a low-cost strategy, or value-based pricing?

- **Sales Channels**: Where and how will customers be able to purchase your product? Will you sell online, through retail stores, or via direct sales?

- **Marketing Tactics**: Describe the specific marketing tactics you'll use to promote your product. This might include digital marketing (SEO, social media, email campaigns), traditional marketing (print ads, events), or partnerships with influencers.

- **Customer Acquisition Strategy**: How do you plan to attract new customers? Will you offer promotions, referral programs, or partnerships?

- **Customer Retention**: What strategies will you use to retain customers and encourage repeat purchases? This might include loyalty programs, subscription models, or personalized offers.

The marketing and sales strategy is one of the most critical sections of your business plan, as it outlines how you'll reach and engage customers. Make sure your strategy is aligned with your target market's preferences and behaviors.

Operations Plan

The operations plan details how your business will run on a day-to-day basis. This section covers everything from production and logistics to staffing and technology. Here's what to include:

- **Production Process**: If you're manufacturing a physical product, describe the production process. Where will your product be made, and what materials or suppliers will you use? What are the timelines for production and delivery?

- **Supply Chain**: Outline your supply chain, including key suppliers, manufacturers, and distribution partners.

- **Technology and Tools**: What technology or tools will you use to run your business? This could include software for inventory management, customer relationship management (CRM), or e-commerce platforms.

- **Staffing Plan**: Provide an overview of your team's structure and the roles you'll need to fill as the business grows. Include details on hiring timelines and any key hires you plan to make.

- **Facilities and Equipment**: If your business requires specific facilities (e.g., a warehouse, office, or manufacturing plant), outline the costs and logistics associated with securing these spaces.

Your operations plan should provide a clear picture of how your business will function on a practical level. It's important to show that you've thought through the logistics and have a plan in place to ensure smooth operations.

Financial Plan

The financial plan is one of the most critical components of your business plan, especially if you're seeking investment. This section provides a detailed projection of your business's financial performance over the next three to five years. Investors will scrutinize this section closely to assess the viability of your business, so it's essential to be thorough and realistic.

Key elements to include are:

- **Revenue Projections**: Provide a breakdown of your expected revenue, including the number of units sold, pricing, and sales channels. Explain any assumptions you've made in your projections, such as market size or growth rate.

- **Cost of Goods Sold (COGS)**: Outline the direct costs associated with producing your product, such as materials, manufacturing, and labor.

- **Operating Expenses**: Include a detailed list of your operating expenses, such as rent, salaries, marketing, and technology.

- **Profit and Loss Statement**: Provide a projected profit and loss (P&L) statement that shows your expected revenue, expenses, and profitability over time.

- **Cash Flow Statement**: A cash flow statement tracks the movement of cash in and out of your business. It's important for showing how you'll manage cash flow, especially in the early stages when expenses may exceed revenue.

- **Break-Even Analysis**: Calculate how many units you need to sell to cover your costs and reach the break-even point.

- **Funding Requirements**: If you're seeking investment or loans, clearly state how much funding you need and how you plan to use it (e.g., for product development, marketing, or hiring).

The financial plan demonstrates that your business is financially viable and that you have a clear path to profitability. Be realistic in your projections and be prepared to explain any assumptions you've made.

Appendix

The appendix is an optional section where you can include additional information that supports your business plan. This might include:

- **Market research data**
- **Product photos or diagrams**
- **Resumes of key team members**
- **Legal documents (e.g., patents or trademarks)**

The appendix provides supplementary information that adds context or credibility to your business plan. While it's not essential, it can be useful for providing investors or partners with additional details.

Conclusion

A well-structured business plan is your roadmap to success. It outlines your goals, strategy, and financial projections, ensuring that you're prepared to navigate the challenges of launching and growing a business. Whether you're seeking investment, partnerships, or simply want to ensure your business is set up for success, a comprehensive business plan provides the clarity and direction you need.

In the next chapter, we'll dive into funding strategies, exploring how to raise capital for your business through various channels, from bootstrapping to venture capital.

Chapter 5: Funding Your Idea: From Bootstrapping to Investors

Every great idea needs resources to bring it to life. Funding is the fuel that helps transform a concept from a spark of inspiration into a tangible product in the marketplace. For most entrepreneurs, securing adequate funding is one of the biggest challenges in launching a business. Whether you're starting small with minimal overhead or looking to scale quickly, the right funding strategy can make the difference between success and failure.

In this chapter, we will explore the different funding options available to entrepreneurs, from self-funding (bootstrapping) to raising capital through investors. We'll discuss the advantages and disadvantages of each method, so you can determine the best path for your business. You'll also learn how to prepare a compelling pitch, create financial projections, and approach potential investors with confidence. Whether you're in the early stages of ideation or ready to scale, this guide will help you navigate the complex world of funding and choose the right strategy for your product journey.

Why Funding Matters

Before we dive into the various funding methods, it's important to understand why securing the right kind of funding is critical. Funding affects many aspects of your business, including:

- **Product Development**: Turning an idea into a market-ready product often requires resources for research, prototyping, testing, and manufacturing.

- **Marketing and Sales**: Once your product is ready, you'll need capital to market it, build brand awareness, and attract customers.

- **Operations**: Funding helps you cover essential operational expenses, such as rent, salaries, technology, and inventory.

- **Growth and Scalability**: If your goal is to grow rapidly, you'll need resources to scale your operations, hire more staff, and enter new markets.

Without sufficient funding, even the most brilliant ideas can stall or fail to gain traction. That's why it's essential to explore different funding options and choose the one that aligns with your business goals and growth strategy.

Bootstrapping: The Self-Funding Route

Bootstrapping refers to the process of funding your business using your own resources, without external investment. This approach allows you to retain full control of your company, but it also requires discipline and careful financial management. Bootstrapping is often the first step for many entrepreneurs, especially those who want to maintain ownership and avoid debt or equity dilution.

Pros of Bootstrapping:

Full Ownership and Control: You don't have to give away equity or answer to investors. Every decision is yours, allowing you to execute your vision without external pressure.

Less Financial Risk: By using your own savings or personal resources, you're not taking on external debt or obligations to repay investors.

Focus on Profitability: Bootstrapping forces you to focus on making your business profitable quickly. Without external funding to fall back on, you're more likely to manage your cash flow effectively and prioritize revenue-generating activities.

Cons of Bootstrapping:

Limited Resources: Without outside funding, you may have fewer resources to invest in product development, marketing, or hiring. This can limit your ability to grow quickly.

Personal Financial Risk: Using your own savings or assets to fund your business can put your personal finances at risk, especially if the business takes longer to become profitable than expected.

Slower Growth: Bootstrapped businesses often grow more slowly because they have to rely on revenue from customers rather than large injections of capital.

When to Bootstrap:

- When your business has low startup costs, and you can manage operations with minimal expenses.
- When you want to maintain full control of your business and avoid giving away equity.
- When your product can generate early revenue to sustain growth.

Strategies for Successful Bootstrapping:

- **Start Small**: Launch with a minimum viable product (MVP) to test the market and generate revenue before investing in more advanced features or scaling.

- **Keep Overheads Low**: Minimize expenses by working from home, outsourcing non-essential tasks, and using cost-effective tools and services.

- **Reinvest Profits**: Instead of taking profits out of the business, reinvest them to fund growth and expansion.

Many successful companies, such as Mailchimp and Spanx, started with bootstrapping. By focusing on profitability and disciplined financial management, these companies grew into industry leaders without ever taking outside investment.

Crowdfunding: Raising Capital from the Crowd

Crowdfunding is a method of raising small amounts of capital from a large number of people, typically via an online platform. This approach has gained popularity in recent years, thanks to platforms like Kickstarter, Indiegogo, and GoFundMe. Crowdfunding allows you to raise money from your target audience and early supporters without giving up equity or taking on debt.

There are two main types of crowdfunding:

Rewards-based crowdfunding: In exchange for financial contributions, backers receive a reward, such as a discount, early access to the product, or exclusive merchandise. This is the most common form of crowdfunding on platforms like Kickstarter.

Equity crowdfunding: In exchange for financial contributions, backers receive equity in your company. Equity crowdfunding is regulated and typically occurs on platforms like SeedInvest or Crowdcube.

Pros of Crowdfunding:

Market Validation: Crowdfunding campaigns allow you to test your product's market demand before committing to full-scale production. If people are willing to fund your product, it's a strong indication that there's demand.

Customer Engagement: Crowdfunding creates a community of early adopters who are invested in your product's success. These backers often become your first customers and brand ambassadors.

No Debt or Equity Dilution (for Rewards-based Crowdfunding): In rewards-based crowdfunding, you're not giving up equity or taking on debt. You're simply pre-selling your product to backers.

Cons of Crowdfunding:

Time-Consuming: Running a successful crowdfunding campaign requires significant time and effort. You'll need to create compelling marketing materials, engage with backers, and manage fulfillment of rewards.

All-or-Nothing Funding (on Some Platforms): On platforms like Kickstarter, if you don't reach your funding goal, you don't receive any funds at all. This can be a risk if you set your goal too high.

Risk of Failure: If your crowdfunding campaign fails to meet its goal, it can signal to investors or partners that there isn't enough market demand for your product.

When to Use Crowdfunding:

- When you have a consumer-facing product that can generate excitement and support from a large audience.

- When you want to test market demand before committing to full production.

- When you need a cash injection for product development or manufacturing without giving up equity.

Strategies for Successful Crowdfunding:

- **Tell a Compelling Story**: Use your crowdfunding campaign to tell the story behind your product. Explain why it matters, how it solves a problem, and why backers should care.

- **Create a Strong Marketing Campaign**: Successful crowdfunding campaigns rely on effective marketing. Build a pre-launch email list, use social media to promote your campaign, and consider working with influencers to spread the word.

- **Set Realistic Goals**: Set a funding goal that's achievable but still enough to cover your production and development costs. Don't overpromise rewards or set timelines that are too ambitious.

Several well-known products, such as the Pebble smartwatch and the Coolest Cooler, began as crowdfunding campaigns that raised millions of dollars from backers. Crowdfunding offers an exciting way to build a community of supporters while raising the funds you need to launch your product.

Friends and Family Funding: Raising Money from Your Network

Another common early-stage funding option is to raise money from friends and family. This method involves borrowing money or selling equity to people within your personal network. Friends and family funding is often a bridge between bootstrapping and more formal investment, providing the capital needed to get your business off the ground.

Pros of Friends and Family Funding:

Quick Access to Capital: Raising money from people you know can be faster and less formal than seeking investment from professional investors or banks.

Favorable Terms: Friends and family may be more willing to offer flexible terms, such as low-interest loans or favorable equity arrangements, because they want to see you succeed.

Support Network: In addition to financial support, friends and family can provide emotional support and encouragement as you build your business.

Cons of Friends and Family Funding:

Risk to Relationships: Mixing personal relationships with financial transactions can be risky. If the business fails or if there's a misunderstanding about repayment, it can strain relationships with friends or family.

Limited Capital: While friends and family may be willing to invest, they likely have limited resources compared to professional investors or venture capitalists. This may not be enough if your business requires significant funding.

Lack of Business Expertise: Unlike professional investors, friends and family may not have experience in evaluating business opportunities. They may not be able to offer valuable advice or guidance as you grow your business.

When to Use Friends and Family Funding:

- When you need a small amount of capital to get your business started, and you have a network of supportive friends or family members.

- When you're not ready to approach professional investors, but you need a cash injection to move forward with product development or marketing.

Strategies for Raising Friends and Family Funding:

- **Be Transparent**: Clearly communicate the risks involved in starting a business. Make sure friends and family understand that there's a chance they may not get their money back.

- **Formalize the Agreement**: Even though you're raising money from people you know, it's important to have a formal agreement in place. This could be a loan agreement with specific repayment terms or an equity agreement if they're buying a stake in your company.

- **Set Clear Expectations**: Make sure everyone is on the same page about how the money will be used, when they can expect to be repaid (if applicable), and what role they will play in the business.

Angel Investors: Early-Stage Equity Investment

Angel investors are individuals who provide early-stage funding to startups in exchange for equity. Angel investors are typically high-net-worth individuals who are willing to take on the risk of investing in new businesses with high growth potential. Unlike venture capitalists, who often invest larger amounts in later-stage companies, angel investors focus on early-stage startups that are still in the process of developing their product or gaining traction.

Pros of Angel Investors:

Significant Funding: Angel investors can provide a significant amount of capital to help you launch or scale your business. This can be especially helpful if your business requires more funding than bootstrapping or crowdfunding can provide.

Mentorship and Guidance: Many angel investors are experienced entrepreneurs themselves, and they often provide valuable advice, mentorship, and connections in addition to funding.

Less Pressure for Immediate Returns: Compared to venture capitalists, angel investors may be more patient with their investments, giving you more time to grow your business before expecting returns.

Cons of Angel Investors:

Equity Dilution: In exchange for funding, you'll need to give up a portion of equity in your company. This means you'll have less ownership and control over the business.

High Expectations: Angel investors typically invest in startups with high growth potential, and they'll expect to see significant returns on their investment. This can create pressure to grow quickly and achieve rapid success.

Finding the Right Investor: Not all angel investors are a good fit for your business. It's important to find an investor who shares your vision and can provide the right kind of support.

When to Seek Angel Investment:

- When you need a significant amount of capital to develop your product, scale your business, or expand into new markets.
- When you want to benefit from an investor's expertise, mentorship, and connections in addition to funding.
- When you're willing to give up equity in exchange for the capital needed to accelerate growth.

Strategies for Securing Angel Investment:

- **Prepare a Strong Pitch**: Angel investors will want to see a compelling pitch that explains your product, market opportunity, business model, and growth potential. Make sure your pitch is clear, concise, and backed by data.

- **Demonstrate Traction**: Angel investors are more likely to invest in startups that have demonstrated some level of traction, whether it's through early sales, customer feedback, or partnerships.
- **Build Relationships**: Angel investment is often based on relationships. Attend networking events, pitch competitions, and industry conferences to connect with potential investors.

Several well-known companies, including Uber and Airbnb, received early-stage funding from angel investors. This type of funding can be a game-changer for startups looking to scale quickly and access valuable resources.

Venture Capital: Scaling with Institutional Investment

Venture capital (VC) is a form of institutional investment that provides large amounts of funding to high-growth startups in exchange for equity. Venture capitalists typically invest in startups that have already demonstrated product-market fit and are looking to scale rapidly. In addition to funding, venture capitalists often provide strategic guidance and access to their networks.

Pros of Venture Capital:

Access to Large Amounts of Capital: Venture capital can provide significant funding to help you scale your business, hire top talent, and enter new markets.

Strategic Support: Venture capitalists often have extensive experience working with startups, and they can provide valuable strategic advice, mentorship, and connections.

Rapid Growth: With the backing of venture capital, you can accelerate your growth and achieve scale much faster than with other funding methods.

Cons of Venture Capital:

Equity Dilution: In exchange for large amounts of capital, you'll need to give up a significant portion of equity. Venture capitalists typically seek ownership stakes that give them influence over the direction of the company.

Pressure for High Growth: Venture capitalists expect rapid growth and high returns on their investment. This can create pressure to scale quickly, even if it means sacrificing profitability or long-term sustainability.

Loss of Control: Depending on the terms of the investment, venture capitalists may take an active role in decision-making. This can reduce your control over the company's direction and strategy.

When to Seek Venture Capital:

- When you have a proven business model, strong traction, and the potential for rapid growth.
- When you need large amounts of capital to scale your business, expand into new markets, or develop new products.
- When you're willing to give up equity and work closely with investors who have a stake in the company's success.

Strategies for Securing Venture Capital:

- **Build a Strong Track Record**: Venture capitalists are more likely to invest in startups that have demonstrated significant traction, such as strong revenue growth, customer acquisition, or strategic partnerships.

- **Target the Right Investors**: Not all venture capitalists are a good fit for your business. Research potential investors to find those who specialize in your industry or have experience working with startups at your stage of growth.

- **Prepare for Due Diligence**: Venture capitalists will conduct extensive due diligence before making an investment. Be prepared to provide detailed financials, market research, and legal documents.

Companies like Facebook, Google, and Amazon all received venture capital funding during their early stages, allowing them to scale rapidly and become global giants. Venture capital can provide the resources needed to achieve significant growth, but it also comes with high expectations and demands for rapid success.

Preparing to Pitch Your Idea

Whether you're seeking investment from angel investors or venture capitalists, a strong pitch is essential. Your pitch should clearly communicate your vision, market opportunity, business model, and growth potential. Here's how to prepare a compelling pitch:

Know Your Audience

Tailor your pitch to the type of investor you're speaking to. Angel investors may be more interested in your personal story and the problem you're solving, while venture capitalists will focus on the market opportunity and scalability of your business.

Tell a Compelling Story

Your pitch should tell a story that captures the investor's attention. Start by describing the problem your product solves and why it matters. Then, explain how your product is the solution and why it's different from what's already available.

Highlight Traction

Investors want to see that your product has traction. This could be in the form of early sales, customer feedback, partnerships, or user engagement. Demonstrating traction shows that there's demand for your product and that you're on the path to success.

Focus on the Market Opportunity

Investors are looking for businesses with significant growth potential. Make sure you clearly explain the size of the market, the demand for your product, and how you plan to capture market share.

Be Prepared with Financial Projections

Investors will want to see detailed financial projections that demonstrate how your business will generate revenue and achieve profitability. Be prepared to explain your revenue model, cost structure, and funding requirements.

Conclusion

Funding is a critical part of turning your idea into a successful product, and there are many paths you can take to secure the resources you need. Whether you choose to bootstrap, crowdfund, seek investment from friends and family, or pursue angel investors or venture capital, the key is to align your funding strategy with your business goals. Each funding method has its own advantages and challenges, so it's important to carefully consider which option is the best fit for your product journey.

In the next chapter, we'll explore the process of branding and positioning your product, so you can create a strong identity that resonates with your target audience and stands out in the market.

Chapter 6: Branding and Positioning: Crafting Your Identity

In a world where thousands of new products are launched every year, having a strong brand is essential to stand out and be memorable. Branding goes far beyond simply choosing a name or designing a logo—it's about creating an identity that resonates with your target audience, communicates your values, and builds long-term trust and loyalty. Whether you're launching a new product or rebranding an existing one, developing a strong brand identity and positioning strategy is critical to your business's success.

Branding is about defining who you are as a company and how you want to be perceived by your customers. It's about the emotions and associations that your product evokes. When done right, branding can turn a simple product into a beloved brand that customers return to again and again. From Apple's sleek, innovative persona to Nike's motivational "Just Do It" mantra, strong brands communicate a clear message and build emotional connections with their audience.

In this chapter, we'll explore the key elements of creating a brand identity, from choosing a name and designing a logo to crafting your brand's message. We'll also delve into the importance of product positioning—how to differentiate your product in a crowded market and ensure it appeals to your target audience. By the end of this chapter, you'll have a clear understanding of how to create a brand that not only stands out but also resonates deeply with your customers.

What is Branding?

Before we dive into the process of creating a brand, it's important to understand what branding actually is. In simple terms, branding is the process of defining and shaping your company's identity and how it is perceived by the world. Your brand encompasses everything from the visual elements like your logo and packaging to the tone of your marketing, the personality of your product, and the emotions you want to evoke in your customers.

A strong brand:

- **Differentiates your product**: In a crowded market, a strong brand helps your product stand out from competitors.

- **Builds recognition and loyalty**: Customers who resonate with your brand are more likely to become repeat buyers and advocates for your product.

- **Communicates your values**: Your brand should reflect the core values of your business, whether that's innovation, sustainability, quality, or affordability.

- **Creates emotional connections**: A successful brand evokes emotions and creates a sense of belonging among customers. People don't just buy products—they buy the experiences and feelings associated with them.

Branding goes beyond aesthetics; it's about the relationship you build with your customers. It's how they perceive your product, what they feel when they interact with it, and what they tell others about their experience. In short, branding is the story you tell, the promise you make, and the emotional journey you take your customers on.

Step 1: Defining Your Brand Identity

The first step in building a successful brand is defining your brand identity. This is the foundation of your branding strategy and sets the tone for everything else, from visual design to marketing. Your brand identity is how you want to be perceived by the world, and it should reflect your company's mission, values, and personality.

Define Your Mission and Vision

Your mission and vision statements are the guiding principles of your brand. They clarify why your company exists, what you aim to achieve, and how you plan to make an impact.

- **Mission Statement**: This defines your company's purpose—why you exist and what problem you are solving. It should be clear, concise, and customer-focused. For example, Patagonia's mission statement is "We're in business to save our home planet," which reflects its commitment to environmental sustainability.

- **Vision Statement**: Your vision is the long-term goal for your company. It's what you aspire to achieve in the future. A strong vision statement is inspirational and gives your company direction. For instance, Tesla's vision is "To accelerate the world's transition to sustainable energy."

By clearly defining your mission and vision, you provide a sense of purpose and direction for your brand. These statements will also guide your decision-making and ensure consistency in your messaging and actions.

Identify Your Core Values

Your brand values are the beliefs and principles that guide your company's behavior. They inform how you interact with customers, employees, and partners, and they help shape your brand's personality. Strong values build trust and loyalty, as customers are more likely to support companies that share their beliefs.

Examples of brand values include:

- **Innovation**: Constantly pushing boundaries and striving to be at the forefront of your industry.

- **Sustainability**: Prioritizing environmentally friendly practices and products.

- **Customer-centricity**: Putting customers first and ensuring their needs and experiences are prioritized.

- **Quality**: Delivering high-quality products that meet or exceed customer expectations.

- **Authenticity**: Being transparent, honest, and true to your brand's promises.

When defining your brand values, think about what principles are most important to your business and how you want to be perceived by your customers. Your values should be reflected in everything you do, from product design to customer service.

Define Your Target Audience

One of the most important aspects of building a brand is understanding who your target audience is. Your brand identity should resonate with your ideal customers and address their specific needs, desires, and pain points. By defining your target audience, you can tailor your messaging, design, and marketing efforts to appeal directly to them.

To define your target audience, consider the following factors:

- **Demographics**: Age, gender, income, education level, geographic location, and occupation.
- **Psychographics**: Values, beliefs, lifestyle, interests, and personality traits.
- **Buying Behavior**: What motivates your customers to make a purchase? What are their buying habits and decision-making processes?

Creating detailed customer personas can help you visualize your target audience. For example, if you're launching a luxury skincare brand, your target audience might be affluent women aged 30-50 who prioritize self-care, quality, and eco-friendly products. By understanding their preferences and behavior, you can create a brand that resonates with them on a personal level.

Determine Your Brand Personality

Just like people, brands have personalities. Your brand personality is the set of human characteristics that define how your brand communicates and interacts with the world.

It shapes the tone and voice of your messaging and influences how customers feel about your product.

There are five main types of brand personalities:

- **Sincerity**: Down-to-earth, honest, wholesome, and cheerful. (e.g., Dove)
- **Excitement**: Daring, imaginative, spirited, and up-to-date. (e.g., Red Bull)
- **Competence**: Reliable, responsible, intelligent, and successful. (e.g., Microsoft)
- **Sophistication**: Elegant, prestigious, luxurious, and refined. (e.g., Chanel)
- **Ruggedness**: Tough, outdoorsy, strong, and rugged. (e.g., Jeep)

When defining your brand personality, think about the type of relationship you want to build with your customers. Are you approachable and friendly, or sophisticated and exclusive? Your personality should be reflected in your messaging, design, and overall brand experience.

Step 2: Choosing a Name for Your Brand

Choosing the right name for your brand is one of the most important decisions you'll make. Your name is the first thing customers will associate with your product, and it needs to be memorable, meaningful, and aligned with your brand identity.

Here are some key considerations when choosing a name:

Keep It Simple and Memorable

Your brand name should be easy to pronounce, spell, and remember. Avoid complex or confusing names that are difficult for customers to recall. Simple names are more likely to stick in people's minds and create a lasting impression.

Examples of simple, memorable brand names include Apple, Nike, and Uber. These names are short, easy to say, and have become synonymous with their respective brands.

Make It Meaningful

Your brand name should reflect your company's mission, values, or the benefits of your product. A meaningful name helps customers understand what your brand stands for and creates an emotional connection.

For example, the name "TOMS" is derived from the word "Tomorrow's Shoes," reflecting the brand's mission to provide shoes to people in need. The name reinforces the company's commitment to social responsibility and resonates with customers who value giving back.

Check Availability

Before finalizing your brand name, make sure it's available for use. Conduct a thorough search to ensure that the name isn't already trademarked or used by another company. You'll also want to check domain name availability for your website and social media handles.

Consider Global Implications

If you plan to expand your brand internationally, make sure your name works in multiple languages and cultures. A name that's appropriate in one country might have a negative or confusing meaning in another, so it's important to do your research to avoid potential issues.

Step 3: Designing Your Logo and Visual Identity

Your logo is one of the most important visual elements of your brand. It serves as a symbol of your brand and is often the first thing customers notice about your product. A well-designed logo communicates your brand's identity, values, and personality in a simple and visually appealing way.

When designing your logo, consider the following factors:

Simplicity and Versatility

A successful logo is simple and versatile. It should be easy to recognize and work across a variety of mediums, from packaging and websites to social media and advertisements. Complex logos with too many details can be difficult to reproduce and may lose clarity when scaled down.

Think about some of the world's most iconic logos—Apple's apple, Nike's swoosh, McDonald's golden arches. These logos are simple, easily recognizable, and work across different platforms.

Color Palette

Colors play a powerful role in branding, as they evoke emotions and associations in the minds of customers. When choosing a color palette for your logo and brand, think about the emotions and values you want to communicate.

Here's a breakdown of common color associations:

- **Red**: Passion, energy, excitement, and urgency (e.g., Coca-Cola, Target)

- **Blue**: Trust, stability, calm, and professionalism (e.g., IBM, Facebook)
- **Green**: Growth, health, nature, and sustainability (e.g., Starbucks, Whole Foods)
- **Yellow**: Optimism, warmth, happiness, and creativity (e.g., McDonald's, Ikea)
- **Black**: Sophistication, luxury, elegance, and authority (e.g., Chanel, Mercedes-Benz)

Choose a color palette that aligns with your brand personality and resonates with your target audience. Your color choices should be consistent across all brand elements, from your logo and website to your packaging and marketing materials.

Typography

The fonts you choose for your logo and brand materials also contribute to your brand's personality. Just like colors, fonts convey specific feelings and associations. For example:

- **Sans-serif fonts** (e.g., Arial, Helvetica) convey a modern, clean, and approachable feel.
- **Serif fonts** (e.g., Times New Roman, Georgia) convey a classic, sophisticated, and formal feel.
- **Script fonts** (e.g., Pacifico, Lobster) convey elegance, creativity, or playfulness.

Your typography should complement your logo and visual identity. Choose fonts that are legible and versatile, as they will be used across multiple platforms and materials.

Logo Variations

It's a good idea to create different versions of your logo for various uses. For example, you might have a primary logo for your website and packaging, a simplified version for social media, and a black-and-white version for print materials. Ensure that all versions of your logo are consistent with your overall brand identity.

Step 4: Crafting Your Brand Message

Your brand message is the way you communicate your values, mission, and unique selling proposition to your audience. It's what sets you apart from competitors and helps customers understand why they should choose your product. A strong brand message is clear, consistent, and resonates with your target audience.

When crafting your brand message, focus on the following elements:

Unique Selling Proposition (USP)

Your USP is what makes your product different from others in the market. It's the reason customers will choose your product over a competitor's. Your USP should be clear, concise, and communicated consistently in all your marketing materials.

For example, Dollar Shave Club's USP is affordability and convenience. Their messaging focuses on delivering quality razors at a fraction of the cost of traditional brands, with the convenience of home delivery.

Brand Promise

Your brand promise is the commitment you make to your customers. It's what they can expect every time they interact with your product. A strong brand promise builds trust and sets customer expectations.

For example, FedEx's brand promise is reliability—"When it absolutely, positively has to be there overnight." This promise reassures customers that they can trust FedEx for timely deliveries.

Tone of Voice

Your brand's tone of voice is how you communicate with your audience. It should be consistent with your brand personality and resonate with your target audience. Whether your tone is formal, casual, witty, or authoritative, it's important to use the same voice across all your communications.

For example, Wendy's social media tone is playful, cheeky, and often humorous, which has helped the brand stand out in the fast-food industry and build a loyal online following.

Tagline

A tagline is a short, memorable phrase that captures the essence of your brand. It reinforces your brand message and helps customers remember what you stand for.

Some iconic taglines include:

- Nike: "Just Do It"
- Apple: "Think Different"
- L'Oréal: "Because You're Worth It"

Your tagline should be easy to remember and encapsulate the core benefit or value of your product.

Step 5: Positioning Your Product in the Market

Once you've built a strong brand identity, the next step is to position your product in the market. Positioning is about defining how your product fits into the competitive landscape and how you want to be perceived relative to your competitors. Effective positioning helps you carve out a unique space in the market and ensures that your product resonates with your target audience.

Identify Your Competitors

Start by identifying your direct and indirect competitors. Direct competitors are companies that offer similar products or services, while indirect competitors offer alternatives that meet the same need in a different way.

For example, if you're launching a plant-based protein bar, your direct competitors might be other plant-based snack brands, while your indirect competitors could include traditional protein bars, energy bars, or meal replacement shakes.

Analyze Your Competitors' Positioning

Study how your competitors are positioning themselves in the market. What messaging do they use? What benefits do they emphasize? How do they appeal to their target audience?

By understanding your competitors' positioning, you can identify gaps or opportunities to differentiate your product. For example, if most of your competitors are focusing on performance and athleticism, you might choose to position your product as more health-conscious or environmentally friendly.

Define Your Positioning Statement

Your positioning statement is a concise summary of how your product is different from competitors and the key benefits it offers to customers. It should clearly communicate your USP and appeal to your target audience.

A typical positioning statement follows this formula:

- **For [Target Audience], [Brand/Product Name]** is the **[Category]** that provides **[Key Benefit]** because **[Reason Why]**.

For example, Volvo's positioning statement might be:

- "For safety-conscious families, Volvo is the car manufacturer that provides the safest driving experience because of its advanced safety features and commitment to innovation."

Your positioning statement serves as a guide for your marketing efforts and ensures that your messaging is consistent and aligned with your brand identity.

Communicate Your Positioning Consistently

Once you've defined your positioning, it's essential to communicate it consistently across all touchpoints. From your website and social media to packaging and advertising, your positioning should be clear and reinforced in every interaction with your brand.

Effective positioning helps customers understand what makes your product unique and why they should choose it over competitors. It also builds trust and reinforces your brand's value proposition.

Step 6: Building Trust and Loyalty

Strong branding is about more than just attracting customers—it's about building long-term trust and loyalty. Brands that consistently deliver on their promises and provide a positive customer experience are more likely to build a loyal customer base. Here's how to build trust and loyalty with your brand:

Deliver Consistent Quality

One of the most important factors in building trust is delivering consistent quality. Customers expect the same level of quality every time they interact with your product. Whether it's the product itself, customer service, or shipping, consistency is key to building trust.

Engage with Your Customers

Engage with your customers regularly to build a sense of community and loyalty. Use social media, email newsletters, and other channels to communicate with your audience, share updates, and respond to feedback.

Building a loyal customer base requires ongoing interaction and relationship-building. Brands that engage with their customers are more likely to foster loyalty and create brand advocates.

Create a Positive Customer Experience

Every interaction with your brand should create a positive experience for customers. This includes everything from how easy it is to navigate your website to the packaging they receive when their order arrives. A great customer experience builds loyalty and encourages repeat purchases.

Reward Loyalty

Loyalty programs, discounts, and exclusive offers are effective ways to reward your most loyal customers. By showing appreciation for their support, you can encourage repeat purchases and foster long-term loyalty.

Conclusion

Branding and positioning are at the heart of creating a successful product. By carefully crafting your brand identity, choosing the right name and logo, and positioning your product in the market, you can build a brand that resonates with your target audience and stands out from competitors. Strong branding creates emotional connections, builds trust, and fosters customer loyalty. In the next chapter, we'll explore marketing strategies to help you build visibility and generate buzz for your product launch.

Chapter 7: Marketing Strategy: Building Buzz and Visibility

Your product is ready to hit the market, but there's one critical question left: How do you ensure that the right people know about it? This is where marketing comes in. A well-crafted marketing strategy is essential for building buzz, creating visibility, and driving sales. Whether you're launching a brand-new product or entering a competitive market, your marketing efforts will determine whether your product gains the attention it deserves.

Marketing is about more than just promoting a product; it's about understanding your target audience, connecting with them through the right channels, and delivering a message that resonates. With the right combination of digital and traditional marketing tactics, you can generate excitement around your product, reach your ideal customers, and build a brand that stands out.

In this chapter, we'll explore a range of marketing strategies, from digital tactics like SEO, social media, and email marketing to traditional approaches like print advertising and public relations. You'll learn how to align your marketing efforts with your business goals, work within your budget, and create a cohesive plan that builds buzz and visibility for your product.

Why a Marketing Strategy is Critical

Marketing is often seen as the bridge between your product and your customers. No matter how innovative or high-quality your product is, it won't succeed if people don't know about it or aren't compelled to buy it. A well-thought-out marketing strategy allows you to:

Reach Your Target Audience: You need to ensure that your marketing efforts are directed toward the people most likely to buy your product. A good marketing strategy identifies the right channels and messaging to connect with your ideal customers.

Build Brand Awareness: Marketing creates visibility for your product, helping it stand out in a crowded market. Through consistent branding and promotion, you can make your product memorable and create a strong brand presence.

Generate Demand and Excitement: Effective marketing doesn't just inform—it excites. By building buzz around your product, you can create anticipation and enthusiasm among potential customers, increasing the likelihood of strong sales from the start.

Measure and Improve: A solid marketing strategy allows you to track the success of your efforts and make adjustments as needed. Whether you're analyzing website traffic, conversion rates, or social media engagement, marketing provides valuable data that helps you refine your approach over time.

Defining Your Marketing Goals

Before diving into specific tactics, it's important to define your marketing goals. These goals will guide your strategy and ensure that your efforts are aligned with your broader business objectives. Marketing goals typically fall into one or more of the following categories:

Brand Awareness

Brand awareness is about getting your product in front of as many people as possible, ensuring that your target audience knows your brand exists. If you're launching a new product or entering a new market, brand awareness is a key objective. Marketing tactics for building brand awareness include social media campaigns, influencer partnerships, public relations, and paid advertising.

Lead Generation

Lead generation focuses on attracting potential customers and capturing their contact information for future follow-up. This is particularly important if you're selling a high-ticket item or if your product requires a longer sales cycle. Tactics for lead generation include content marketing, email sign-ups, webinars, and paid search ads.

Sales and Conversions

If your primary goal is to drive immediate sales, your marketing strategy should focus on conversion-driven tactics. This involves targeting customers who are ready to buy and optimizing your website or online store for conversions. Effective conversion strategies include retargeting ads, special offers, and creating a sense of urgency with limited-time deals.

Customer Retention and Loyalty

Marketing isn't just about acquiring new customers; it's also about keeping the ones you have. Customer retention and loyalty programs focus on nurturing relationships with existing customers to encourage repeat purchases and build long-term loyalty. Tactics for this include email marketing, loyalty programs, and personalized offers.

Once you've defined your marketing goals, you can begin building a strategy that aligns with your business objectives. Keep in mind that your goals may evolve over time, so be prepared to adjust your strategy as your business grows.

Crafting Your Marketing Message

Your marketing message is the core idea or value proposition that you want to communicate to your audience. It's the reason why customers should choose your product over others and the story you tell to connect with them emotionally. Crafting a compelling marketing message is essential for capturing attention and driving engagement.

When developing your marketing message, consider the following elements:

Identify Your Unique Selling Proposition (USP)

Your USP is what sets your product apart from competitors. It's the specific benefit or feature that makes your product unique and valuable to your target audience. Whether it's a technological innovation, superior quality, or a lower price point, your USP should be central to your marketing message.

For example, if your product is an eco-friendly alternative to traditional cleaning products, your USP might be, "A natural, non-toxic cleaner that's safe for your family and the environment."

Focus on Benefits, Not Features

While it's important to highlight your product's features, your marketing message should focus on the benefits those features provide. Customers care more about how your product will improve their lives or solve a problem than they do about technical specifications.

For example, instead of saying, "Our vacuum has a powerful 1200-watt motor," focus on the benefit: "Our vacuum cleans your home in half the time, leaving you more time to relax."

Speak to Your Target Audience's Pain Points

Understanding your target audience's needs, desires, and pain points is crucial for crafting a message that resonates. What problem does your product solve for them? How does it make their life easier or better? By addressing these pain points directly, you can create a message that feels personal and relevant.

Use Emotion to Create Connection

People don't just buy products; they buy the feelings and experiences associated with those products. Effective marketing messages evoke emotion, whether it's excitement, joy, trust, or a sense of belonging. Think about the emotional impact you want your product to have and incorporate that into your messaging.

Once you've developed your core marketing message, ensure that it's consistent across all your marketing channels. Whether it's on your website, social media, or advertising, your message should be clear, concise, and aligned with your brand identity.

Digital Marketing Strategies

In today's digital world, having a strong online presence is essential for building buzz and visibility. Digital marketing offers a wide range of tools and tactics to reach your audience, engage with potential customers, and drive sales. Let's explore some of the most effective digital marketing strategies you can use to promote your product.

Search Engine Optimization (SEO)

Search engine optimization (SEO) is the process of optimizing your website and content to rank higher in search engine results pages (SERPs). When your website appears at the top of search results for relevant keywords, it increases visibility, drives organic traffic, and builds credibility.

Here are the key components of SEO:

- **Keyword Research**: Identify the keywords and phrases your target audience is searching for. Use tools like Google Keyword Planner or Ahrefs to find high-volume, low-competition keywords related to your product.

- **On-Page SEO**: Optimize your website's content, title tags, meta descriptions, and headings for your target keywords. Make sure your content is clear, informative, and valuable to readers.

- **Technical SEO**: Ensure that your website is fast, mobile-friendly, and easy to navigate. Search engines prioritize websites that provide a positive user experience.

- **Content Marketing**: Regularly publish high-quality, relevant content (such as blog posts, guides, or videos) that provides value to your audience and incorporates your target keywords.

SEO is a long-term strategy that requires consistent effort, but it's one of the most cost-effective ways to build organic traffic and visibility over time.

Social Media Marketing

Social media platforms like Facebook, Instagram, Twitter, LinkedIn, and TikTok are powerful tools for building brand awareness, engaging with your audience, and driving traffic to your website. Social media marketing involves creating and sharing content that resonates with your audience, whether it's product updates, behind-the-scenes looks, user-generated content, or promotions.

Here are some tips for effective social media marketing:

- **Choose the Right Platforms**: Focus on the social media platforms where your target audience is most active. For example, if you're targeting millennials or Gen Z, platforms like Instagram and TikTok may be more effective than LinkedIn or Twitter.

- **Create Engaging Content**: Social media is all about engagement. Create content that encourages likes, comments, shares, and conversations. Use a mix of content formats, such as images, videos, polls, and stories, to keep your audience engaged.

- **Use Hashtags and Tags**: On platforms like Instagram and Twitter, hashtags help increase the discoverability of your posts. Use relevant hashtags to reach a wider audience. Tagging other brands, influencers, or partners can also help boost visibility.

- **Run Paid Ads**: Social media platforms offer powerful advertising tools that allow you to target specific demographics, interests, and behaviors.

Running paid ads on platforms like Facebook or Instagram can help you reach new audiences, drive traffic, and increase conversions.

Social media marketing allows you to connect with your audience in real-time, build relationships, and create a community around your brand.

Email Marketing

Email marketing remains one of the most effective ways to nurture leads, drive sales, and build customer loyalty. With email marketing, you can deliver personalized, relevant messages directly to your audience's inbox, whether you're promoting a new product, offering a discount, or sharing valuable content.

Here's how to build a successful email marketing strategy:

- **Build an Email List**: Start by collecting email addresses from your website visitors, customers, and social media followers. Offer incentives, such as a discount or free resource, to encourage sign-ups.

- **Segment Your List**: Divide your email list into segments based on factors like purchase history, interests, or engagement level. This allows you to send targeted emails that are more likely to resonate with each group.

- **Create Compelling Content**: Your email content should provide value to your audience. Whether it's product updates, exclusive offers, or educational content, make sure your emails are engaging, relevant, and aligned with your brand message.

- **Use Automation**: Email automation allows you to send timely, personalized emails based on triggers like sign-ups, purchases, or abandoned carts. For example, you can set up a welcome email series for new subscribers or a post-purchase follow-up email for customers.

Email marketing is a cost-effective way to maintain ongoing communication with your audience, build relationships, and drive repeat sales.

Influencer Partnerships

Influencer marketing involves partnering with individuals who have a large and engaged following on social media or other online platforms. Influencers can help you reach new audiences, build credibility, and create buzz around your product.

Here's how to approach influencer marketing:

- **Identify Relevant Influencers**: Look for influencers who align with your brand values and have an audience that matches your target market. You don't need to partner with celebrities—micro-influencers (those with smaller but highly engaged audiences) can be just as effective.

- **Build Authentic Partnerships**: Work with influencers who genuinely love your product and are excited to share it with their audience. Authentic partnerships feel more genuine to followers and lead to better results.

- **Create Engaging Campaigns**: Collaborate with influencers to create content that showcases your product in an authentic and engaging way. Whether it's a product review, a sponsored post, or a giveaway, make sure the content is compelling and relevant to the influencer's audience.

Influencer marketing can be a powerful way to leverage the trust and credibility that influencers have built with their followers.

Traditional Marketing Strategies

While digital marketing is essential in today's world, traditional marketing tactics can still play a valuable role in building buzz and visibility. Depending on your product and target audience, a mix of digital and traditional strategies can help you reach a wider audience and create a more well-rounded marketing approach.

Public Relations (PR)

Public relations involves managing your brand's reputation and building relationships with the media to gain positive coverage. A strong PR strategy can help you get your product featured in newspapers, magazines, blogs, and TV shows, creating valuable exposure and credibility.

Here's how to build a successful PR strategy:

- **Create a Press Kit**: A press kit is a collection of materials that journalists can use to write about your product. It typically includes a press release, product information, high-quality images, and company background.

- **Build Relationships with Journalists**: Reach out to journalists and bloggers who cover your industry or target audience. Personalize your pitch, explain why your product is relevant to their readers, and offer to send a sample or arrange an interview.

- **Leverage Events and Launches**: Hosting an event or product launch can generate media attention and give journalists an opportunity to experience your product firsthand. Whether it's a virtual event or an in-person gathering, make sure to invite media and influencers who can help spread the word.

PR can help build credibility and trust by getting your product in front of reputable media outlets and influencers.

Print Advertising

While digital ads are increasingly popular, print advertising can still be effective, particularly if your target audience engages with magazines, newspapers, or trade publications. Print ads allow you to reach a more niche or local audience and can be a great complement to your digital efforts.

Here's how to use print advertising effectively:

- **Choose the Right Publications**: Focus on publications that are relevant to your industry or audience. For example, if you're selling a fitness product, advertising in a health and wellness magazine might be a good fit.

- **Create Eye-Catching Ads**: Your print ad should be visually appealing and include a clear call to action. Make sure the design reflects your brand identity and captures the attention of readers.

- **Track Results**: While print ads are harder to track than digital ads, you can include a unique discount code or a dedicated landing page to measure how many customers are coming from your print ads.

Print advertising can be particularly effective for luxury brands, local businesses, or products that benefit from visual storytelling.

Event Marketing

Event marketing involves promoting your product through in-person or virtual events, such as trade shows, pop-up shops, workshops, or product demos. Events give you the opportunity to showcase your product, connect with customers, and build relationships in a more personal and interactive way.

Here's how to use event marketing effectively:

- **Attend Industry Trade Shows**: Trade shows and industry conferences are a great way to get your product in front of potential buyers, partners, and media. Make sure to create an engaging booth that showcases your product and encourages interaction.

- **Host Pop-Up Shops**: If you're selling a physical product, a pop-up shop allows you to create a temporary retail space where customers can experience your product firsthand. This can generate buzz and create a sense of exclusivity.

- **Offer Workshops or Demos**: Hosting a workshop or demo allows you to educate your audience and showcase the value of your product. For example, if you're launching a new kitchen gadget, you could host a cooking demo to show how it works in real-time.

Event marketing allows you to create memorable experiences that leave a lasting impression on potential customers.

Paid Advertising Strategies

Paid advertising is a fast and effective way to reach your target audience, drive traffic, and generate sales. Whether you're running digital ads on social media or buying ad space in a magazine, paid advertising allows you to reach new customers and promote your product to a larger audience.

Pay-Per-Click (PPC) Advertising

Pay-per-click (PPC) advertising involves placing ads on search engines like Google and Bing, where you only pay when someone clicks on your ad. PPC ads appear at the top of search results for specific keywords, making them a powerful way to reach customers who are actively searching for products like yours.

Here's how to run successful PPC campaigns:

- **Conduct Keyword Research**: Use tools like Google Keyword Planner to identify the most relevant and high-traffic keywords for your product.

- **Write Compelling Ad Copy**: Your ad copy should clearly communicate your USP and include a strong call to action. Make sure it's relevant to the keywords you're targeting.

- **Optimize Your Landing Pages**: When someone clicks on your ad, they should be directed to a landing page that matches the message of your ad and makes it easy for them to take the next step, whether that's making a purchase or signing up for more information.

PPC advertising can deliver immediate results by driving targeted traffic to your website and converting searchers into customers.

Social Media Ads

Social media platforms like Facebook, Instagram, and LinkedIn offer highly targeted advertising options that allow you to reach specific demographics, interests, and behaviors. Social media ads can help you build brand awareness, drive website traffic, and increase conversions.

Here's how to run successful social media ad campaigns:

- **Define Your Target Audience**: Use the targeting options on social media platforms to reach specific groups of people based on demographics, interests, and behaviors.

- **Create Engaging Visuals**: Social media ads are highly visual, so make sure your images or videos are eye-catching and aligned with your brand.

- **Use Retargeting**: Retargeting ads allow you to show ads to people who have already visited your website or engaged with your brand. These ads are highly effective for converting warm leads into customers.

Social media ads are a cost-effective way to reach new audiences and drive conversions, especially when combined with organic social media marketing.

Measuring and Optimizing Your Marketing Efforts

One of the key advantages of digital marketing is the ability to track and measure your efforts in real-time. By monitoring key performance indicators (KPIs), you can assess the success of your marketing campaigns and make data-driven decisions to optimize your strategy.

Here are some KPIs to track:

- **Website Traffic**: Use tools like Google Analytics to track how much traffic your website is receiving and where it's coming from (e.g., social media, search engines, email).

- **Conversion Rate**: Measure the percentage of website visitors who take a desired action, such as making a purchase or signing up for your email list.

- **Click-Through Rate (CTR)**: Track the percentage of people who click on your ads or email links to gauge how well your messaging is resonating with your audience.

- **Return on Investment (ROI)**: Calculate the ROI of your marketing campaigns by comparing the revenue generated to the cost of the campaign.

By regularly reviewing your KPIs, you can identify what's working, what's not, and where you should focus your marketing efforts to get the best results.

Conclusion

A well-crafted marketing strategy is essential for building buzz, creating visibility, and driving sales for your product.

By combining digital marketing tactics like SEO, social media, and email marketing with traditional approaches like PR, print ads, and events, you can reach your target audience and create a lasting impact. Remember to define your marketing goals, craft a compelling message, and track your results to optimize your efforts over time.

In the next chapter, we'll dive into production and scaling, exploring how to move from prototype to mass production and build a supply chain that supports your growth.

Chapter 8: Production and Scaling: From Prototype to Mass Production

You've developed a prototype, gathered feedback, and your product has attracted interest from potential customers or investors. Now comes a critical phase in your entrepreneurial journey: production. Taking your product from a working prototype to mass production is a complex process that requires careful planning, coordination, and execution. It involves finding reliable manufacturers, building an efficient supply chain, maintaining quality control, and scaling up production to meet demand. Getting this phase right is essential to ensuring that your product reaches the market smoothly, on time, and within budget.

This chapter will guide you through the process of moving from prototype to mass production. We'll explore how to choose the right manufacturing partners, manage costs, and set up systems that allow your business to scale. You'll also learn about the challenges of scaling production, the importance of maintaining quality control, and how to avoid common pitfalls that can derail your production efforts.

The Transition from Prototype to Production

Prototyping allows you to test your product, gather feedback, and refine the design, but the transition from prototype to production is a major shift. Prototypes are often handcrafted or produced in small batches, whereas mass production requires scaling up to larger volumes, managing complex processes, and working with external suppliers or manufacturers. This transition involves several key steps:

1. **Refining the Product Design for Manufacturing**
2. **Choosing a Manufacturing Partner**
3. **Setting Up a Supply Chain**
4. **Establishing Quality Control Systems**
5. **Managing Production Costs**

Let's explore each of these steps in detail.

Refining the Product Design for Manufacturing

Before you can move to mass production, your product design needs to be optimized for manufacturing. A prototype might work well as a small-scale version of your product, but mass production requires designs that are cost-effective, reliable, and easy to reproduce at scale.

Design for Manufacturing (DFM)

Design for Manufacturing (DFM) is the process of modifying your product design to make it easier and more cost-effective to manufacture. This often involves simplifying the design, choosing the right materials, and ensuring that the product can be assembled efficiently.

Here are some key principles of DFM:

- **Simplify the Design**: The more complex a product is, the more expensive and difficult it will be to manufacture. Look for ways to reduce the number of components, simplify assembly, and eliminate unnecessary features.

- **Choose Cost-Effective Materials**: While your prototype might have used high-end or custom materials, these may not be practical for mass production. Work with your manufacturer to identify materials that offer the right balance of quality, durability, and cost.
- **Standardize Components**: Whenever possible, use standard components that are readily available and easy to source. Custom components can increase production costs and lead times.
- **Optimize for Assembly**: Make sure your product is easy to assemble at scale. Consider how parts will be put together and whether assembly can be automated to reduce labor costs.

Creating Technical Drawings and Documentation

Once your design has been optimized for manufacturing, you'll need to create detailed technical drawings and documentation. These documents serve as the blueprint for your manufacturer and include precise measurements, material specifications, and assembly instructions. Clear and accurate documentation is essential for ensuring that your product is manufactured consistently and meets your quality standards.

Your documentation should include:

- **CAD (Computer-Aided Design) Files**: Detailed 3D models of your product, including dimensions, materials, and tolerances.
- **Bill of Materials (BOM)**: A comprehensive list of all the components and materials needed to produce your product, including quantities and suppliers.

- **Assembly Instructions**: Step-by-step instructions for assembling the product, including any tools or equipment needed.

Choosing a Manufacturing Partner

Finding the right manufacturing partner is one of the most important decisions you'll make in the production process. A reliable manufacturer can help you produce high-quality products on time and within budget, while a poor choice can lead to delays, quality issues, and increased costs.

Here are the key factors to consider when choosing a manufacturer:

Domestic vs. Overseas Manufacturing

One of the first decisions you'll need to make is whether to manufacture domestically or overseas. Each option has its own advantages and challenges.

- **Domestic Manufacturing**: Manufacturing in your home country offers several benefits, including shorter lead times, easier communication, and greater control over quality. However, domestic manufacturing is often more expensive than overseas options, especially for labor-intensive products.

- **Overseas Manufacturing**: Manufacturing overseas, particularly in countries like China, Vietnam, or India, can significantly reduce production costs. However, it can also introduce challenges such as longer lead times, language barriers, and potential quality control issues.

When deciding between domestic and overseas manufacturing, consider the following factors:

- **Cost**: Labor and production costs are typically lower overseas, but shipping, tariffs, and potential quality issues can offset these savings.

- **Lead Time**: Domestic manufacturers often offer faster turnaround times, while overseas production may take longer due to shipping and customs delays.

- **Quality Control**: If maintaining high-quality standards is critical to your product, domestic manufacturing may offer greater control and easier oversight.

- **Communication**: Time zone differences, language barriers, and cultural differences can make communication with overseas manufacturers more challenging.

Evaluating Potential Manufacturers

Once you've decided where you want to manufacture, you'll need to evaluate potential partners. Look for manufacturers that have experience producing similar products and can meet your volume, quality, and timeline requirements.

Here's how to evaluate potential manufacturers:

- **Experience and Expertise**: Does the manufacturer have experience producing products like yours? Do they specialize in your industry or product category?

- **Capacity**: Can the manufacturer handle the volume of production you need? Make sure they have the capacity to scale up production as your business grows.

- **Reputation and Reliability**: Research the manufacturer's reputation by reading reviews, asking for references, and checking their track record with other clients. Reliability is key—late deliveries or quality issues can harm your business.
- **Quality Standards**: Does the manufacturer have a strong quality control process? Ask about their certifications (such as ISO 9001) and how they ensure that products meet specifications.
- **Communication and Responsiveness**: Good communication is essential for a successful manufacturing partnership. Make sure the manufacturer is responsive and easy to work with, especially if you're managing production remotely.

Requesting Quotes and Samples

Before committing to a manufacturer, request quotes from multiple suppliers. The quote should include all production costs, including materials, labor, tooling, and shipping. Compare the quotes to ensure you're getting the best value for your budget.

In addition to quotes, request samples from potential manufacturers. This allows you to evaluate the quality of their work and ensure that the manufacturer can produce your product to your specifications. Be thorough in testing the samples for functionality, durability, and overall quality.

Setting Up a Supply Chain

Once you've chosen a manufacturer, you'll need to set up a supply chain to manage the flow of materials, components, and products from suppliers to your production facility and, ultimately, to your customers. A well-organized supply chain is essential for ensuring that production runs smoothly and that you can scale up as demand grows.

Sourcing Materials and Components

If your product requires specific materials or components that aren't supplied by your manufacturer, you'll need to establish relationships with suppliers. This includes sourcing raw materials (such as metals, plastics, or fabrics) as well as any custom components that are part of your product.

Here's how to source materials and components effectively:

- **Identify Reliable Suppliers**: Look for suppliers that have a strong reputation for quality and reliability. You'll need to ensure that they can deliver materials consistently and on time.

- **Negotiate Pricing**: Work with suppliers to negotiate bulk pricing for materials and components. The more you can order in larger quantities, the lower your per-unit costs will be.

- **Establish Lead Times**: Make sure you understand each supplier's lead times for delivery and build these timelines into your production schedule. Delays in receiving materials can disrupt your entire production process.

Managing Inventory

As you scale up production, managing inventory becomes increasingly important. You'll need to strike a balance between keeping enough inventory on hand to meet demand

and avoiding overproduction, which can lead to excess stock and increased storage costs.

Here are some key inventory management strategies:

- **Just-in-Time (JIT) Inventory**: JIT inventory management involves keeping minimal inventory on hand and ordering materials or components only as needed. This reduces storage costs and waste but requires precise coordination with suppliers to avoid production delays.

- **Safety Stock**: Safety stock is extra inventory that you keep on hand to protect against unexpected demand spikes or supply chain disruptions. While safety stock adds to your inventory costs, it can prevent stockouts and lost sales.

- **Inventory Tracking Systems**: Invest in an inventory management system to track your stock levels, monitor supplier deliveries, and manage reorders. This helps ensure that you always have the materials and components you need for production without overstocking.

Logistics and Shipping

Shipping logistics are a critical part of your supply chain, especially if you're working with overseas manufacturers or distributing products to customers worldwide. You'll need to coordinate shipping from your manufacturer to your warehouse or fulfillment center, as well as the final delivery to customers.

Here are some logistics considerations:

- **Shipping Costs**: Shipping can add significant costs to your production process, especially for bulky or heavy products. Make sure you factor shipping costs into your pricing strategy.

- **Customs and Duties**: If you're manufacturing overseas, you'll need to navigate customs regulations and duties. Work with a customs broker or logistics partner to ensure that your products clear customs smoothly.

- **Lead Times**: Shipping lead times can vary depending on the origin and destination of your products. Plan your production schedule around these lead times to avoid delays.

Establishing Quality Control Systems

Maintaining consistent product quality is essential for building customer trust and ensuring long-term success. Quality control involves monitoring and testing your products at various stages of the production process to ensure they meet your specifications and standards.

Setting Quality Standards

Before production begins, establish clear quality standards for your product. These standards should cover:

- **Materials**: The specific materials and components that will be used in production, including their quality, durability, and performance.

- **Dimensions and Tolerances**: The precise measurements and tolerances for each component of the product. Tolerances define the allowable variation in dimensions without affecting the product's performance.

- **Performance and Functionality**: Any performance criteria that your product must meet, such as strength, durability, or functionality under specific conditions.

- **Aesthetic Standards**: The appearance of your product, including color, finish, and texture.

Document these standards and communicate them clearly to your manufacturer. This ensures that both parties have a shared understanding of what constitutes an acceptable product.

Inspection and Testing

Quality control inspections and testing should be conducted at multiple stages of production to catch any issues early and prevent defects from reaching customers.

Here are some common quality control methods:

- **Incoming Material Inspections**: Inspect raw materials and components as they arrive from suppliers to ensure they meet your specifications before they are used in production.

- **In-Process Inspections**: Conduct inspections during the production process to identify and address any issues before the product is completed. This can include checking dimensions, assembly, and functionality.

- **Final Product Inspections**: Inspect the finished product to ensure it meets all quality standards before it is packaged and shipped. This can include performance testing, visual inspections, and functional tests.

Third-Party Quality Control

If you're manufacturing overseas or working with a large-scale production facility, you may want to hire a third-party quality control service to conduct inspections on your behalf. Third-party inspectors provide an unbiased assessment of product quality and can help ensure that your manufacturer is meeting your standards.

Managing Production Costs

Production costs can quickly add up, and managing these costs effectively is critical to maintaining profitability. As you scale up production, you'll need to carefully monitor expenses and find ways to reduce costs without sacrificing quality.

Cost of Goods Sold (COGS)

Your cost of goods sold (COGS) includes all the direct costs associated with producing your product, such as materials, labor, and manufacturing overhead. Reducing your COGS can increase your profit margins and give you more flexibility in pricing.

Here are some ways to reduce your COGS:

- **Negotiate with Suppliers**: As you scale up production, leverage your increased order volumes to negotiate lower prices with suppliers. Bulk purchasing can lead to significant cost savings.

- **Optimize Production Processes**: Look for ways to streamline your production process and reduce labor costs. This could involve automating certain tasks, improving assembly efficiency, or eliminating unnecessary steps.

- **Reduce Waste**: Minimize waste during production by optimizing material usage and improving manufacturing precision. Reducing waste not only lowers costs but also supports sustainability efforts.

Budgeting for Production Costs

When scaling up production, it's important to create a detailed production budget that accounts for all costs, including materials, labor, shipping, and overhead. This budget should be realistic and based on accurate estimates from your suppliers and manufacturers.

Here are some key costs to include in your production budget:

- **Material Costs**: The cost of raw materials and components, including any shipping or handling fees.

- **Manufacturing Costs**: The cost of labor, machinery, and overhead at your manufacturing facility.

- **Tooling Costs**: If your product requires custom molds, dies, or other tooling, factor these costs into your budget.

- **Shipping and Logistics Costs**: The cost of shipping materials to your manufacturer and finished products to your warehouse or customers.

- **Quality Control Costs**: The cost of inspections, testing, and any third-party quality control services.

Regularly review your production budget to ensure that costs are staying within your projections. If costs are rising, work with your manufacturer or suppliers to find ways to reduce expenses without compromising quality.

Scaling Up for Demand

As demand for your product grows, you'll need to scale up your production to keep up. Scaling production involves increasing your manufacturing capacity, expanding your supply chain, and ensuring that you can meet customer demand without compromising quality or efficiency.

Increasing Manufacturing Capacity

If your current manufacturer can't handle increased production volumes, you may need to find additional manufacturers or invest in new equipment to increase capacity.

Here's how to scale your manufacturing capacity:

- **Work with Multiple Manufacturers**: If your current manufacturer can't handle the volume, consider working with additional manufacturers to distribute the production load. This can also provide backup options in case of disruptions.

- **Invest in Automation**: Automating certain parts of the production process can help you increase output and reduce labor costs. Work with your manufacturer to identify areas where automation can improve efficiency.

- **Plan for Seasonal or Peak Demand**: If your product experiences seasonal demand fluctuations, plan your production schedule to accommodate these peaks. This might involve increasing production in advance or working with temporary manufacturing partners.

Expanding Your Supply Chain

As production scales, your supply chain will also need to grow to ensure that you have access to the materials, components, and logistics support needed to meet demand. This might involve expanding your network of suppliers, optimizing inventory management, and working with additional logistics partners.

Maintaining Quality as You Scale

Scaling production can introduce challenges in maintaining consistent product quality. As you increase production volumes, there's a greater risk of defects, delays, and quality issues. To maintain quality as you scale, focus on:

- **Continuous Quality Control**: Ensure that quality control measures are scaled along with production. This may involve hiring additional quality control staff or increasing the frequency of inspections.

- **Training and Oversight**: As production scales, make sure that your manufacturing partners have the necessary training and oversight to maintain quality standards. Regularly review their performance and address any issues promptly.

- **Customer Feedback**: Monitor customer feedback and reviews to identify any quality issues that arise as production scales. Use this feedback to improve your processes and prevent future problems.

Conclusion

Scaling your product from prototype to mass production is a complex and challenging process, but with the right approach, it can be done efficiently and effectively. By optimizing your product design for manufacturing, choosing reliable partners, and setting up a robust supply chain, you can ensure that your production process runs smoothly and meets customer demand. Quality control, cost management, and the ability to scale are all critical to long-term success, and this phase of your business will lay the foundation for future growth.

In the next chapter, we'll explore the importance of customer feedback and iteration. You'll learn how to use customer insights to continually improve your product and adapt to changing market needs.

Chapter 9: Distribution Channels: Getting Your Product to Market

Once your product is ready for mass production, the next critical step is ensuring that it reaches your customers efficiently and cost-effectively. No matter how innovative or well-designed your product is, it won't succeed if it doesn't reach the right people at the right time. This is where distribution channels come into play. The distribution strategy you choose will significantly impact your business's growth, profitability, and customer satisfaction.

A strong distribution strategy includes selecting the right channels to sell your product, managing logistics and fulfillment efficiently, and ensuring a smooth customer experience from order to delivery. This chapter will guide you through the process of getting your product to market, covering various distribution models, including direct-to-consumer (DTC), retail partnerships, e-commerce platforms, and wholesale opportunities. You'll also learn how to manage logistics, shipping, and fulfillment while keeping costs low and customer satisfaction high.

The Importance of Choosing the Right Distribution Channels

Your choice of distribution channels can make or break your product's success. The right channel allows you to reach your target audience, create a seamless purchasing experience, and maintain profitability. Conversely, the wrong channel can lead to high costs, poor customer experiences, and limited market reach.

Here's why selecting the right distribution channels is essential:

Reaching Your Target Audience: Different distribution channels cater to different customer segments. For example, young, tech-savvy consumers might prefer to shop online, while others may prefer the tactile experience of purchasing in-store. Your distribution channels should align with where your target audience shops.

Maximizing Profitability: Each distribution channel has its own cost structure, from shipping fees to retail markups. Understanding the costs associated with each channel allows you to maintain healthy profit margins.

Building Brand Awareness: Certain distribution channels, such as retail partnerships or e-commerce platforms like Amazon, can help increase your brand's visibility. The more places your product is available, the more customers will recognize and trust your brand.

Scalability: Some distribution channels are better suited for scaling your business as demand grows. For instance, e-commerce platforms can help you scale faster by reaching a global audience, while retail partnerships may require more resources to expand.

Types of Distribution Channels

There are several distribution channels to choose from, each with its advantages and challenges. The key is to select the channel—or combination of channels—that best aligns with your business goals, target market, and resources. Let's explore the most common distribution channels and how they can help you get your product to market.

Direct-to-Consumer (DTC)

Direct-to-consumer (DTC) is a business model where you sell your product directly to your customers without intermediaries. This model has become increasingly popular with the rise of e-commerce, as it allows businesses to maintain control over their brand and customer relationships.

Benefits of DTC:

- **Higher Profit Margins**: By cutting out the middleman (such as retailers or distributors), you can keep a larger share of the profit. You don't have to pay retail markups or share revenue with third parties.

- **Control Over Branding**: When you sell directly to consumers, you have full control over the customer experience, from the website design to the packaging. This allows you to create a cohesive brand image and message.

- **Direct Customer Relationships**: Selling DTC gives you access to valuable customer data, such as purchasing habits, preferences, and feedback. This data can help you refine your product, improve customer service, and build loyalty.

Challenges of DTC:

- **Marketing and Customer Acquisition**: Without the support of retailers or distributors, you're responsible for driving traffic to your website and acquiring customers. This requires a robust marketing strategy and budget.

- **Logistics and Fulfillment**: Managing logistics, shipping, and returns can be complex, especially as your business grows. You'll need to invest in a reliable fulfillment infrastructure to ensure timely deliveries and handle customer service effectively.

How to Succeed with DTC:

- **Build a User-Friendly E-Commerce Site**: Your website is your storefront, so it should be easy to navigate, visually appealing, and optimized for conversions. Invest in a responsive design, clear product descriptions, high-quality images, and a seamless checkout process.

- **Invest in Digital Marketing**: Since you won't have the support of retail partners to drive sales, you'll need to invest in digital marketing to reach your target audience. Focus on SEO, social media marketing, paid ads, and email campaigns to attract and convert customers.

- **Optimize Fulfillment**: Partner with a reliable fulfillment provider or set up an in-house system to manage inventory, shipping, and returns efficiently. A smooth fulfillment process is crucial for maintaining customer satisfaction and encouraging repeat purchases.

Retail Partnerships

Retail partnerships involve selling your product through brick-and-mortar stores or online retailers. This channel allows you to tap into the retailer's customer base and benefit from their marketing and distribution infrastructure.

Benefits of Retail Partnerships:

- **Increased Brand Exposure**: Retailers have established customer bases, and getting your product on their shelves can significantly increase your visibility and credibility. Consumers often trust products sold in reputable stores, which can enhance your brand's reputation.

- **Access to Larger Audiences**: Retailers, especially large chains, give you access to a much broader customer base than you might be able to reach on your own. This is particularly useful for scaling your business.

- **Shared Marketing and Distribution Costs**: Retailers often handle much of the marketing and distribution efforts, which can reduce your operational costs and logistical challenges.

Challenges of Retail Partnerships:

- **Lower Profit Margins**: Retailers typically mark up the price of your product, meaning you'll receive a smaller percentage of the sale price. You may also need to offer retailers discounts or promotions to get your product featured prominently.

- **Loss of Control**: Once your product is in a retailer's hands, you have less control over how it's displayed, marketed, and sold. This can make it difficult to maintain consistency in branding and customer experience.

- **Retailer Requirements**: Large retailers often have strict requirements for suppliers, including minimum order quantities, pricing structures, and packaging standards. Meeting these requirements can be challenging for small businesses.

How to Succeed with Retail Partnerships:

- **Research Potential Retailers**: Before approaching a retailer, make sure their target audience aligns with your product. Consider starting with smaller, independent retailers to gain experience and build your brand before pursuing larger chains.

- **Negotiate Favorable Terms**: When working with retailers, negotiate terms that protect your profit margins and ensure fair pricing. Be prepared to offer discounts or promotions to secure shelf space, but make sure the terms are sustainable for your business.

- **Provide Strong Marketing Support**: Even though retailers handle much of the marketing, you can still provide support to help boost sales. Offer in-store promotions, signage, or branded displays to attract attention to your product.

E-Commerce Platforms

E-commerce platforms like Amazon, eBay, Etsy, and Shopify offer a powerful way to reach a global audience and sell your product online. These platforms provide the infrastructure for online sales, including payment processing, customer service tools, and fulfillment options.

Benefits of E-Commerce Platforms:

- **Global Reach**: E-commerce platforms allow you to reach customers around the world, expanding your market far beyond your local area.

- **Ease of Setup**: Platforms like Shopify and Etsy are designed to be user-friendly, allowing you to set up an online store quickly and start selling your product without the need for technical expertise.

- **Built-In Traffic**: Popular platforms like Amazon have millions of users searching for products every day. Listing your product on these platforms gives you access to this built-in audience, increasing the chances of discovery.

Challenges of E-Commerce Platforms:

- **Competition**: E-commerce platforms are highly competitive, with thousands of similar products available. Standing out and attracting customers requires strong marketing, competitive pricing, and excellent reviews.

- **Fees and Commissions**: E-commerce platforms typically charge fees or commissions on each sale, which can eat into your profit margins. Be sure to factor these costs into your pricing strategy.

- **Platform Dependence**: Selling on third-party platforms means you're subject to their rules and policies. Changes in platform algorithms, fees, or policies can impact your sales and profitability.

How to Succeed on E-Commerce Platforms:

- **Optimize Product Listings**: Your product listings should include high-quality images, clear descriptions, and relevant keywords to improve visibility and attract customers. Be sure to highlight the unique features and benefits of your product.

- **Encourage Customer Reviews**: Positive reviews are critical for building trust and driving sales on e-commerce platforms. Encourage satisfied customers to leave reviews and respond promptly to any negative feedback.

- **Offer Competitive Pricing**: Pricing is a major factor in e-commerce sales. Research your competitors and set a price that offers value to customers while maintaining profitability.

Wholesale Opportunities

Wholesale involves selling your product in bulk to other businesses, such as retailers, distributors, or resellers, who then sell it to the end consumer. This model allows you to sell large quantities of your product at once, generating steady revenue and reducing the need for direct-to-consumer marketing.

Benefits of Wholesale:

- **Large Order Volumes**: Wholesale allows you to sell your product in bulk, which can generate significant revenue and help you clear inventory quickly.

- **Long-Term Partnerships**: Building relationships with wholesalers, retailers, or distributors can lead to long-term, repeat business, providing a steady source of income.

- **Reduced Marketing Efforts**: Since wholesalers handle the distribution and sales to the end consumer, you don't need to invest as heavily in marketing or customer acquisition.

Challenges of Wholesale:

- **Lower Profit Margins**: Wholesale typically involves selling your product at a lower price than retail, as your customers (the wholesalers or retailers) need to mark it up to make a profit.

- **Payment Terms**: Wholesale transactions often involve extended payment terms, meaning you may not receive payment for your products until weeks or months after delivery.

- **Inventory Management**: Selling in large volumes can lead to inventory challenges, especially if your production process isn't yet optimized for high-volume orders.

How to Succeed in Wholesale:

- **Offer Attractive Pricing and Terms**: Wholesalers expect to purchase your product at a lower price than the retail price, so offer competitive pricing while ensuring that your margins remain sustainable. You may also need to offer flexible payment terms to attract wholesale customers.

- **Build Strong Relationships**: Wholesale relationships are built on trust and reliability. Ensure that you deliver on your promises and maintain open communication with your wholesale partners.

- **Attend Trade Shows**: Trade shows are a great way to connect with potential wholesale buyers, showcase your product, and build relationships with distributors and retailers. Prepare a professional presentation and have samples available to attract interest.

Managing Logistics, Shipping, and Fulfillment

Effective logistics, shipping, and fulfillment are essential for delivering your product to customers on time and in good condition. Whether you're managing fulfillment in-house or working with third-party logistics (3PL) providers, it's crucial to streamline these processes to keep costs low and maintain high customer satisfaction.

In-House Fulfillment

In-house fulfillment means that you handle all aspects of order processing, inventory management, packing, and shipping. This option gives you full control over the fulfillment process but can be resource-intensive as your business grows.

Benefits of In-House Fulfillment:

- **Full Control**: You have complete control over the fulfillment process, allowing you to ensure that orders are packed correctly, shipped on time, and meet your quality standards.
- **Cost Savings (at Small Scale)**: If you're managing a small number of orders, in-house fulfillment can be cost-effective, as you won't need to pay fees to a third-party provider.

Challenges of In-House Fulfillment:

- **Resource-Intensive**: As your order volume grows, managing fulfillment in-house can become time-consuming and require additional staff, warehouse space, and equipment.

- **Scaling Limitations**: In-house fulfillment can limit your ability to scale quickly, especially if you lack the infrastructure to handle large volumes of orders efficiently.

How to Succeed with In-House Fulfillment:

- **Invest in Inventory Management Software**: Use inventory management software to track stock levels, process orders, and manage shipping efficiently. This helps prevent stockouts and ensures that orders are processed quickly.

- **Optimize Packing and Shipping**: Streamline your packing and shipping process by organizing your inventory, using efficient packaging materials, and partnering with reliable shipping carriers.

- **Prepare for Growth**: As your business grows, evaluate whether in-house fulfillment is still the best option. You may need to invest in additional staff, warehouse space, or automation to keep up with demand.

Third-Party Logistics (3PL)

Third-party logistics (3PL) providers handle the entire fulfillment process on your behalf, including warehousing, packing, and shipping orders. Partnering with a 3PL allows you to scale your fulfillment operations without investing in additional infrastructure or staff.

Benefits of 3PL:

- **Scalability**: 3PL providers are equipped to handle large volumes of orders and can scale with your business as demand grows. This allows you to focus on other aspects of your business without worrying about fulfillment.

- **Reduced Overhead**: By outsourcing fulfillment to a 3PL, you eliminate the need for warehouse space, packing materials, and additional staff, reducing your operational costs.

- **Faster Shipping**: Many 3PL providers have multiple fulfillment centers across different regions, allowing them to ship orders faster and reduce delivery times.

Challenges of 3PL:

- **Less Control**: Outsourcing fulfillment means that you have less control over the packing and shipping process. If your 3PL provider makes a mistake, it can impact your customers' experience.

- **Fees and Costs**: While 3PL can reduce overhead, it comes with fees for storage, packing, and shipping. These costs can add up, so it's important to ensure that the benefits of outsourcing outweigh the fees.

How to Succeed with 3PL:

- **Choose the Right Provider**: Not all 3PL providers are the same. Choose a provider that has experience in your industry, can handle your product's specific requirements (such as fragile or perishable items), and offers competitive pricing.

- **Monitor Performance**: Even though you're outsourcing fulfillment, it's important to monitor your 3PL provider's performance. Track order accuracy, shipping times, and customer feedback to ensure they're meeting your standards.

- **Maintain Clear Communication**: Establish clear communication channels with your 3PL provider to ensure that any issues are addressed quickly and that they have the information they need to fulfill orders accurately.

Hybrid Fulfillment

Some businesses use a hybrid fulfillment model, where they manage a portion of their orders in-house while outsourcing the rest to a 3PL provider. This approach allows you to maintain control over certain orders while benefiting from the scalability of a 3PL for larger volumes.

How to Succeed with Hybrid Fulfillment:

- **Segment Orders**: Use in-house fulfillment for high-priority or custom orders that require a personal touch, while outsourcing standard orders to a 3PL provider. This allows you to focus on customer experience while keeping costs low.
- **Coordinate Inventory**: Ensure that your inventory management system is integrated with both your in-house and 3PL fulfillment operations. This prevents stockouts and ensures that orders are fulfilled from the correct location.

Keeping Costs Low While Ensuring Customer Satisfaction

Managing the costs of distribution, shipping, and fulfillment is critical to maintaining profitability. However, it's equally important to ensure that customers have a positive experience with your brand. Here's how to strike the right balance between cost-efficiency and customer satisfaction:

Optimize Shipping Costs

Shipping can be one of the most significant costs in your distribution strategy, especially if you're selling physical products. Here are some ways to optimize shipping costs:

- **Negotiate with Carriers**: If you're shipping large volumes, negotiate bulk discounts with shipping carriers. You may also be able to secure lower rates by partnering with a 3PL provider that has relationships with major carriers.

- **Offer Multiple Shipping Options**: Give customers the option to choose between standard, expedited, and free shipping (if feasible). Offering free shipping for orders over a certain amount can encourage larger purchases.

- **Use Flat-Rate Shipping**: Flat-rate shipping options can help reduce shipping costs for heavier items and simplify the checkout process for customers.

Streamline Fulfillment

Efficient fulfillment is key to keeping costs low and ensuring that customers receive their orders on time. Here are some tips for streamlining your fulfillment operations:

- **Automate Order Processing**: Use software to automate order processing, inventory tracking, and shipping label generation. This reduces manual errors and speeds up the fulfillment process.

- **Choose the Right Packaging**: Use packaging that fits your product's dimensions to reduce shipping costs and avoid wasted materials. Lightweight packaging can also help lower shipping fees.

- **Monitor Fulfillment Performance**: Regularly track key metrics such as order accuracy, shipping times, and customer satisfaction. This allows you to identify areas for improvement and address any issues before they impact your bottom line.

Focus on Customer Service

Exceptional customer service is essential for building loyalty and encouraging repeat purchases. Here's how to ensure that customers have a positive experience with your brand:

- **Provide Transparent Shipping Information**: Let customers know when to expect their orders by providing tracking information and clear delivery estimates.

- **Offer Hassle-Free Returns**: Make it easy for customers to return or exchange products by offering a simple returns process and prepaid return shipping labels.

- **Respond Quickly to Issues**: If a customer has a problem with their order, respond promptly and offer a solution. Great customer service can turn a negative experience into a positive one.

Conclusion

Selecting the right distribution channels is a critical part of bringing your product to market and scaling your business. Whether you choose to sell directly to consumers, partner with retailers, leverage e-commerce platforms, or explore wholesale opportunities, each channel comes with its own benefits and challenges. By carefully evaluating your options, managing logistics efficiently, and maintaining high customer satisfaction, you can create a distribution strategy that maximizes reach, minimizes costs, and sets your product up for long-term success.

In the next chapter, we'll explore customer feedback and iteration, focusing on how to use customer insights to refine your product, improve the customer experience, and drive continuous improvement.

Chapter 10: Measuring Success and Iteration: Continuous Improvement

Bringing a product to market is a monumental achievement, but it is by no means the end of the road. In fact, it's just the beginning. Once your product is out in the world, the real work of measuring success and refining your offering begins. It's not enough to simply launch a product and hope for the best—staying competitive in a dynamic marketplace requires constant evaluation, learning, and iteration.

In this chapter, we'll explore how to measure the success of your product using a variety of tools and metrics, including sales data, customer feedback, and market response. More importantly, you'll learn how to use this data to inform continuous improvements to your product. The ability to adapt and iterate based on real-world feedback is one of the most critical skills for long-term success in business. By continually refining your product, improving the customer experience, and responding to changes in the market, you can keep your business competitive and ensure sustainable growth.

Why Measuring Success is Critical

Success in business is not static. The market is always evolving, competitors are constantly innovating, and customer preferences can shift overnight. Measuring success is not just about looking at the immediate results of a product launch; it's about understanding the ongoing performance of your product in the market and identifying opportunities for improvement.

Here are some key reasons why measuring success is essential:

Identify What's Working: By analyzing your product's performance, you can identify which aspects of your business strategy are working well—whether it's a marketing campaign, pricing strategy, or product feature. This allows you to double down on successful tactics and refine less effective ones.

Uncover Problems Early: Continuous measurement allows you to catch issues before they become major problems. Whether it's a quality issue, shipping delays, or customer dissatisfaction, early detection gives you the chance to address these challenges before they damage your reputation or sales.

Drive Product Improvement: Measuring success provides you with the data you need to improve your product. Customer feedback, in particular, can reveal valuable insights into how you can make your product better, whether by adding new features, improving usability, or addressing pain points.

Adapt to Market Changes: The business landscape is constantly changing, and what works today may not work tomorrow. Regularly measuring success helps you stay agile and respond to new trends, competitor strategies, or shifts in consumer behavior.

Key Metrics for Measuring Product Success

There are numerous metrics you can track to measure your product's success, but it's important to focus on the ones that are most relevant to your business goals. These metrics can be broken down into three main categories: sales data, customer feedback, and market response.

Sales Data

Sales data is one of the most direct indicators of your product's success. By tracking your sales performance, you can understand how well your product is being received by the market, identify trends over time, and assess the effectiveness of your marketing and distribution strategies.

Here are some key sales metrics to track:

- **Revenue**: Your total sales revenue is a primary indicator of your product's success. Track revenue over time to see whether it's increasing, staying flat, or declining. Compare actual revenue to your forecasts to assess whether your product is meeting expectations.

- **Sales Growth Rate**: The sales growth rate shows how quickly your revenue is increasing (or decreasing) over time. A high growth rate indicates strong demand, while a stagnant or negative growth rate may signal that your product is losing momentum.

- **Units Sold**: Tracking the number of units sold helps you understand demand for your product. This metric is particularly useful for identifying trends related to seasonality, promotions, or market shifts.

- **Average Order Value (AOV)**: AOV measures the average amount customers spend per order. Increasing your AOV can boost revenue without necessarily increasing the number of customers, and it's often achieved by upselling or cross-selling additional products.

- **Customer Acquisition Cost (CAC)**: CAC measures how much it costs to acquire a new customer. By comparing your CAC to your customer's lifetime value (LTV), you can determine whether you're spending too much to acquire new customers or if your marketing efforts are yielding a positive return.

Tracking these sales metrics gives you a clear picture of your product's financial performance, but it's important to dig deeper into what's driving these numbers. For example, if your revenue is growing but your AOV is declining, you might need to adjust your pricing strategy or introduce new product bundles to increase order size.

Customer Feedback

Sales data can tell you how well your product is selling, but it doesn't tell you why customers are buying it—or not buying it. This is where customer feedback comes in. Customer feedback provides invaluable insights into the customer experience, helping you understand what's working, what's not, and where there are opportunities for improvement.

Here are some ways to collect and analyze customer feedback:

- **Surveys**: Customer surveys are a great way to gather direct feedback on your product. Ask customers about their overall satisfaction, what they like and dislike about the product, and any suggestions they have for improvement. You can send surveys after a purchase, following customer support interactions, or at key milestones in the customer journey.

- **Net Promoter Score (NPS)**: NPS measures customer loyalty by asking customers how likely they are to recommend your product to others. NPS is a strong indicator of customer satisfaction and brand loyalty, and it can help you gauge whether your product is building long-term relationships with customers.

- **Product Reviews and Ratings**: Online reviews and ratings provide real-time feedback on your product from customers. Pay close attention to common themes in the reviews—both positive and negative—as they can highlight areas where your product is excelling or falling short.

- **Social Media Listening**: Social media platforms are a valuable source of customer feedback. By monitoring mentions of your brand or product on platforms like Twitter, Instagram, and Facebook, you can gain insights into what customers are saying, whether they're satisfied, and how they're interacting with your brand.

Market Response

Market response refers to how your product is being received by the broader market, including competitors, industry trends, and external factors. By analyzing market response, you can identify opportunities for growth, as well as potential threats from competitors or changes in consumer behavior.

Here's how to measure market response:

- **Market Share**: Your market share represents the percentage of total sales in your industry or category that your product captures. Tracking your market share over time helps you understand how well your product is performing relative to competitors.

- **Competitor Analysis**: Regularly monitor your competitors to see how their products are performing, what strategies they're using, and how their offerings compare to yours. This can help you identify gaps in the market or areas where your product could be improved.

- **Industry Trends**: Stay up-to-date with industry trends and developments that may impact your product. This could include changes in consumer preferences, technological advancements, or regulatory shifts. Adapting your product to align with market trends can help you stay competitive and meet evolving customer needs.

Iteration: How to Improve Your Product Based on Feedback

Once you've gathered sales data, customer feedback, and market insights, the next step is to use this information to improve your product. Iteration is the process of making continuous, incremental improvements to your product based on real-world data and feedback. This approach allows you to refine your offering, address customer pain points, and stay ahead of competitors.

Here's how to approach iteration in a structured and effective way:

Prioritize Areas for Improvement

Not all feedback is created equal, and it's important to prioritize which issues to address first. Start by categorizing feedback into three main categories: critical issues, nice-to-have improvements, and new feature requests.

- **Critical Issues**: These are problems that significantly impact the customer experience, such as bugs, usability issues, or product defects. Addressing these issues should be your top priority, as they can directly affect customer satisfaction and retention.

- **Nice-to-Have Improvements**: These are suggestions that could enhance the customer experience but aren't necessarily critical. Examples might include small design changes or additional color options. While these improvements aren't urgent, they can help differentiate your product from competitors.

- **New Feature Requests**: Customers often provide ideas for new features or capabilities they'd like to see in your product. While it's important to consider these requests, be mindful of feature creep (adding too many unnecessary features). Focus on features that align with your product's core value proposition and will have the most significant impact.

By categorizing feedback, you can focus your resources on the changes that will have the greatest positive effect on your product and customer satisfaction.

Test and Validate Changes

Once you've identified areas for improvement, the next step is to test and validate changes before fully rolling them out. This ensures that your changes will have the desired effect and that you're not introducing new issues.

Here are some methods for testing and validating product changes:

- **A/B Testing**: A/B testing involves creating two versions of your product or feature and testing them with different segments of your audience. By comparing the performance of each version, you can determine which one leads to better results. For example, if you're testing a new checkout process, you can create two versions and measure which one leads to higher conversion rates.

- **Beta Testing**: Beta testing involves releasing a new version of your product to a small group of users before rolling it out to the general public. This allows you to gather feedback from real users in a controlled environment and identify any issues before a full release.

- **Customer Feedback Loops**: Keep customers in the loop by asking for feedback after you've made changes. This could involve sending follow-up surveys or monitoring customer satisfaction scores to see how the changes are impacting the customer experience.

Implement Changes Gradually

Rather than making sweeping changes to your product all at once, implement improvements gradually. This approach allows you to monitor the impact of each change and make adjustments as needed. It also reduces the risk of overwhelming your customers with too many changes at once, which can lead to confusion or dissatisfaction.

Start by rolling out small improvements that address the most critical issues, then gradually introduce new features or enhancements based on customer feedback. By taking a measured approach, you can ensure that each iteration leads to tangible improvements without disrupting the overall customer experience.

Iterate on Your Business Model and Strategy

Iteration doesn't just apply to your product—it also applies to your business model, marketing strategy, and overall operations. As you gather more data and learn more about your customers and market, be prepared to make adjustments to how you sell, market, and deliver your product.

For example, if you notice that certain customer segments are responding particularly well to your product, consider tailoring your marketing efforts to focus on these segments. If you find that your pricing strategy is limiting sales growth, you might experiment with different pricing models, such as subscription plans or bundled offers.

The key is to remain flexible and open to change. The businesses that succeed in the long run are those that can adapt and evolve based on real-world data and feedback.

Staying Competitive Through Continuous Improvement

The most successful businesses are those that embrace continuous improvement and iteration as part of their culture. Staying competitive in a fast-changing market requires an ongoing commitment to evaluating your product, listening to your customers, and making data-driven decisions to enhance your offering.

Here's how to foster a culture of continuous improvement in your business:

Create a Feedback Loop

Establish a continuous feedback loop that allows you to gather, analyze, and act on customer feedback regularly. This can be done through surveys, product reviews, social media monitoring, and customer support interactions. Make it easy for customers to provide feedback and let them know that their opinions are valued.

Set Clear Goals and KPIs

Set clear, measurable goals for product improvement based on the data you collect. For example, if customer satisfaction scores are lower than expected, set a goal to improve them by a specific percentage over the next quarter. Track key performance indicators (KPIs) such as NPS, customer retention rates, and product return rates to monitor progress.

Encourage Experimentation

Innovation often comes from experimentation and a willingness to take calculated risks. Encourage your team to test new ideas, whether it's a new feature, marketing tactic, or operational improvement. Create a culture where failure is seen as a learning opportunity, and celebrate successes when experiments lead to positive results.

Monitor Competitors and Industry Trends

Keep an eye on your competitors and stay informed about industry trends. This can help you identify opportunities for differentiation or improvement. For example, if a competitor launches a new feature that resonates with customers, evaluate whether a similar feature could enhance your product—or whether you can offer an even better solution.

Build Customer Loyalty Through Continuous Improvement

Customers appreciate businesses that listen to their feedback and make improvements based on their needs. By consistently iterating on your product and improving the customer experience, you can build strong relationships with your customers and foster long-term loyalty.

Conclusion

Measuring success and iterating on your product is a never-ending process, but it's one that pays off in the long run. By continuously evaluating your product's performance, gathering customer feedback, and making data-driven improvements, you can stay competitive, build a loyal customer base, and drive sustainable growth for your business.

In the final chapter, we'll explore how to maintain and scale your business over the long term, ensuring that your product and brand continue to thrive in an ever-changing market.

Conclusion: The Journey Ahead: Embracing Innovation and Growth

Congratulations! You've completed the journey from idea to a market-ready product, navigating the complex steps of ideation, prototyping, production, distribution, and iteration. You've learned how to define and refine your product, bring it to market, and measure its success. But while this is a major accomplishment, it's essential to recognize that the entrepreneurial journey doesn't end here. In many ways, the work is just beginning.

The world of business and innovation is constantly evolving, and long-term success depends on your ability to continue growing, learning, and adapting. Markets shift, customer needs change, and new competitors emerge. Staying ahead of the curve requires more than just a great product—it requires a mindset of continuous innovation, a willingness to embrace failure, and the courage to take calculated risks.

In this conclusion, we'll reflect on the mindset and strategies necessary for long-term success. You'll discover the importance of staying agile, learning from both successes and failures, and maintaining a focus on growth. Ultimately, the key to thriving in today's dynamic market is to view the journey as ongoing—a never-ending process of improvement, evolution, and reinvention.

Embracing a Mindset of Continuous Innovation

In the fast-paced business world, standing still is not an option. Products that succeed today can quickly become obsolete tomorrow, and businesses that fail to innovate risk falling behind. Continuous innovation is the key to staying relevant, meeting evolving customer needs, and creating new opportunities for growth.

Innovation as a Core Value

To truly embrace innovation, it must become a core value of your business. Innovation shouldn't just be something you focus on during product development—it should be an ongoing process that informs every aspect of your business. This includes not only improving your product but also innovating in areas such as marketing, customer service, operations, and business strategy.

When innovation is embedded in your company culture, it encourages everyone in the organization to think creatively, challenge the status quo, and find new ways to solve problems. This mindset leads to constant improvement and helps your business remain competitive in a rapidly changing market.

Staying Customer-Centric

At the heart of continuous innovation is a deep understanding of your customers. Innovation should always be driven by customer needs and desires, not just by technology or trends. By staying closely connected to your customers and listening to their feedback, you can identify new opportunities for innovation that will truly resonate with them.

Some of the most successful innovations are born out of a desire to solve specific customer pain points. For example, the rise of subscription services in industries ranging from fashion to technology was driven by customers' desire for convenience and personalization. Companies that can anticipate and respond to these needs are better positioned to innovate in meaningful ways.

Leveraging Technology for Innovation

In today's digital age, technology plays a pivotal role in driving innovation. Whether it's leveraging artificial intelligence to personalize customer experiences, using data analytics to make more informed business decisions, or embracing automation to streamline operations, technology offers countless opportunities to innovate and stay competitive.

However, it's important to remember that technology is not a goal in itself—it's a tool that should be used to enhance your business and better serve your customers. The most successful businesses are those that use technology to solve real-world problems and deliver tangible value.

Fostering a Culture of Experimentation

Innovation often requires experimentation and the willingness to take risks. In a culture of continuous innovation, failure is not something to be feared—it's an opportunity to learn and grow. Encouraging a culture of experimentation allows your team to test new ideas, learn from failures, and refine their approach.

For example, Google is known for its "20% time" policy, which encourages employees to spend 20% of their work time on side projects that interest them. This policy has led to the development of innovative products like Gmail and Google Maps. By fostering a culture where experimentation is valued, you create an environment where breakthrough ideas can emerge.

Learning from Failures: The Path to Success

Failure is an inevitable part of the entrepreneurial journey, but it's also one of the most valuable learning experiences. Every entrepreneur faces setbacks, whether it's a product that doesn't perform as expected, a marketing campaign that falls flat, or a partnership that doesn't work out. The key to long-term success is not avoiding failure but learning from it and using those lessons to improve.

Reframing Failure as a Learning Opportunity

One of the most important shifts in mindset you can make as an entrepreneur is to reframe failure as a learning opportunity. When things don't go as planned, take the time to analyze what went wrong and why. Did you misread the market? Was there a flaw in the product design? Did you underestimate your competitors?

By taking a proactive approach to failure, you can turn setbacks into valuable insights that inform your future decisions. For example, Airbnb's founders faced numerous rejections and challenges in their early days, but instead of giving up, they used each setback as an opportunity to refine their business model and improve their platform. Today, Airbnb is a global success story, largely because the founders were willing to learn from their failures.

Failing Fast and Iterating Quickly

In the world of innovation, the concept of "failing fast" is often championed as a way to accelerate learning and improvement. The idea is to test new ideas quickly, learn from the results, and iterate based on what you've learned. This approach allows you to make adjustments early on, before investing too much time or money into an idea that may not work.

Failing fast doesn't mean being reckless—it means being willing to take calculated risks, gather feedback, and make adjustments as you go. By iterating quickly and learning from each failure, you can refine your product, improve your processes, and increase your chances of success.

Building Resilience and Perseverance

The ability to bounce back from failure is a key trait of successful entrepreneurs. Resilience and perseverance are essential qualities for navigating the ups and downs of the business world. When faced with failure, it's important to maintain a positive mindset, stay focused on your long-term vision, and continue pushing forward.

One of the best ways to build resilience is to surround yourself with a strong support network. Whether it's mentors, advisors, or fellow entrepreneurs, having people to turn to for guidance and encouragement can help you stay motivated during challenging times.

Staying Agile in a Changing Market

The business landscape is constantly evolving, and staying agile is critical to long-term success. Agility means being able to respond quickly to changes in the market, adapt to new trends, and pivot your business strategy when necessary. In today's fast-paced world, businesses that can stay nimble and flexible are better positioned to seize new opportunities and navigate challenges.

Monitoring Market Trends

Staying on top of market trends is essential for maintaining agility. This involves regularly monitoring changes in customer behavior, technological advancements, and shifts in the competitive landscape. By keeping a close eye on these trends, you can identify new opportunities for innovation and stay ahead of the curve.

For example, the rise of e-commerce has drastically changed the retail landscape, and businesses that were quick to adapt by building online stores or offering digital services were able to thrive. Similarly, companies that can identify emerging technologies—such as artificial intelligence, blockchain, or the Internet of Things—can position themselves as leaders in their industry.

Being Willing to Pivot

Sometimes, despite your best efforts, your original business strategy may not work as planned. When this happens, it's important to be willing to pivot—changing your approach based on new information or market conditions.

A famous example of a successful pivot is Instagram, which started as a location-based social networking app called Burbn. After realizing that users were primarily interested in the app's photo-sharing features, the founders pivoted to focus exclusively on photo sharing, which eventually led to Instagram becoming the global platform it is today.

Pivoting doesn't mean abandoning your vision—it means adapting your strategy to better align with market demand and customer needs.

Adopting an Agile Business Model

Agile business models prioritize flexibility, responsiveness, and customer-centricity. This approach, which originated in software development, can be applied to all areas of your business. Agile businesses focus on delivering value to customers through short, iterative cycles, allowing them to adapt quickly to feedback and market changes.

In practice, this might involve regularly releasing updates to your product based on customer feedback, testing new marketing strategies in small batches, or experimenting with new business models. By adopting an agile approach, you can stay responsive to the market and continuously improve your offering.

Cultivating Long-Term Growth and Sustainability

While innovation and agility are essential for short-term success, long-term growth requires a commitment to sustainability—both in terms of your business practices and your growth strategy. Sustainable growth is about scaling your business in a way that is financially viable, socially responsible, and environmentally conscious.

Scaling Your Business Sustainably

Scaling too quickly can lead to growing pains, such as cash flow issues, supply chain bottlenecks, or quality control problems. To ensure sustainable growth, it's important to scale at a pace that your business can handle. This means carefully managing your resources, maintaining high standards of quality, and ensuring that your infrastructure can support increased demand.

Focus on building a strong foundation for growth by investing in scalable systems, developing a talented team, and fostering strong relationships with suppliers, partners, and customers.

Fostering Customer Loyalty

Long-term growth is built on customer loyalty. While acquiring new customers is important, retaining existing customers is often more cost-effective and leads to higher lifetime value. To foster customer loyalty, focus on delivering exceptional value, providing outstanding customer service, and building meaningful relationships with your audience.

Offering loyalty programs, personalized experiences, and consistent communication can help deepen your connection with customers and encourage repeat business.

Commitment to Sustainability and Social Responsibility

Today's consumers are increasingly conscious of the environmental and social impact of the businesses they support. Companies that prioritize sustainability and social responsibility not only attract loyal customers but also contribute to a better world.

Consider ways to make your business more sustainable, whether through eco-friendly packaging, ethical sourcing, or reducing your carbon footprint. Additionally, aligning your business with a social cause that resonates with your audience can strengthen your brand and build a deeper emotional connection with customers.

Continuing to Push Boundaries and Take Risks

The entrepreneurial journey is one of constant exploration, learning, and growth. As you look to the future, remember that the most successful entrepreneurs are those who continue to push boundaries, take risks, and challenge themselves to think bigger.

Setting Ambitious Goals

Setting ambitious goals is one of the best ways to keep your business moving forward. These goals should be bold but achievable, and they should inspire both you and your team to reach for new heights. Whether it's launching a new product line, expanding into international markets, or reaching a specific revenue target, having a clear vision for the future will help keep you focused and motivated.

Embracing Risk with Confidence

Risk is an inherent part of entrepreneurship, and while it can be daunting, it's also where the greatest rewards lie. The key to managing risk is to approach it with confidence and preparation. Take calculated risks by conducting thorough research, analyzing potential outcomes, and making informed decisions.

Remember, even if a risk doesn't pay off as expected, the experience often leads to valuable insights and opportunities for growth. The most successful entrepreneurs are those who are willing to step outside their comfort zones and take risks in pursuit of their vision.

Inspiring Others on the Journey

As you continue to grow and evolve as an entrepreneur, don't forget the impact you can have on others. Whether through mentorship, sharing your experiences, or contributing to your community, your journey can inspire others to pursue their own entrepreneurial dreams. By paying it forward and helping others along the way, you not only contribute to the success of others but also strengthen your own sense of purpose and fulfillment.

Final Thoughts: The Journey Never Ends

The entrepreneurial journey is not a destination—it's a continuous path of growth, innovation, and discovery. While you've achieved a significant milestone by taking an idea from inception to market, your work is far from over. The key to long-term success lies in your ability to stay adaptable, embrace change, and keep pushing forward.

As you move forward, remember that every challenge is an opportunity, every failure is a lesson, and every success is a stepping stone toward even greater achievements. Keep your eyes open for new opportunities, stay connected to your customers, and never stop learning.

Most importantly, enjoy the journey. The process of turning ideas into reality is one of the most rewarding and fulfilling experiences you can have as an entrepreneur. Embrace the highs and the lows, the successes and the failures, and continue to push the boundaries of what's possible.

Your journey has only just begun.

In this book, you've learned how to bring an idea to life, from brainstorming and prototyping to scaling and iterating. Now, as you move forward, use these tools and strategies to keep innovating, evolving, and growing your business. The future is full of possibilities, and with the right mindset and approach, there's no limit to what you can achieve.

Best of luck on your journey ahead! Keep dreaming big, take risks, and continue to turn your ideas into successful ventures.

Appendix: 50 Simple Ideas that Made Huge Profits

You don't have to invent a complex engineering device to power the world's energy needs to make money. History proves that sometimes the simplest ideas are the best. Here's a list of 60 simple inventions that became incredibly profitable:

1. **Paperclips** – Wire bent into a loop to hold paper.

2. **Post-it Notes** – Simple sticky paper notes.

3. **Rubber Bands** – Simple elastic loops.

4. **Pet Rock** – A rock marketed as a pet.

5. **Pool Noodles** – Foam tubes used for swimming.

6. **Frisbee** – A simple flying disc.

7. **Clothes Hanger** – Wire or plastic hanger for clothes.

8. **Velcro** – Hook-and-loop fastener.

9. **Slinky** – A toy that moves down stairs.

10. **Band-Aids** – Adhesive bandages for small cuts.

11. **Q-tips** – Cotton swabs for cleaning.

12. **Hula Hoop** – Plastic hoop used as a toy.

13. **Glow Sticks** – Simple light sources used at parties.

14. **Plastic Cup** – Disposable drinking cups.

15. **Koozie** – Insulated holder for cans or bottles.

16. **Toothpicks** – Small sticks for cleaning teeth.

17. **Earplugs** – Small foam or silicone plugs for hearing protection.

18. **Bobby Pins** – Small hairpins used in styling.

19. **Can Opener** – Basic tool for opening cans.

20. **Bubble Wrap** – Packing material with air pockets.

21. **Bic Pens** – Cheap disposable ballpoint pens.

22. **Ziplock Bags** – Resealable plastic bags.

23. **Silicone Wristbands** – Popularized by the Livestrong campaign.

24. **Tupperware** – Plastic food storage containers.

25. **Yo-Yo** – Classic toy that has seen multiple revivals.

26. **Crocs** – Foam clogs.

27. **Snuggie** – A blanket with sleeves.

28. **Mood Rings** – Rings that change color based on body temperature.

29. **Fidget Spinner** – A small toy designed to reduce stress.

30. **Koosh Ball** – A soft, stretchy ball toy.

31. **The Chia Pet** – A small, decorative plant.

32. **Super Soaker** – High-powered water gun.

33. **Silly Putty** – A stretchy, bouncy material.

34. **Magic 8-Ball** – A fortune-telling toy.

35. **PopSockets** – Phone grips that pop out.

36. **Sticky Hands** – Stretchy toys that stick to surfaces.

37. **Whoopee Cushion** – A classic prank item.

38. **Loom Bands** – Small elastic bands used to make bracelets.

39. **Potato Peeler** – Simple kitchen tool.

40. **Waterproof Earbuds** – For swimming or workouts.

41. **Popsicle** – Frozen treat on a stick.

42. **Keychain Flashlight** – Small flashlight for keychains.

43. **Stretch Armstrong** – Stretchable action figure toy.

44. **Wite-Out** – Correction fluid for mistakes on paper.

45. **Nerf Ball** – Soft foam ball.

46. **Twist Tie** – Simple wire ties for closing bags.

47. **Umbrella** – A simple rain protection device.

48. **Kleenex** – Disposable facial tissues.

49. **Rubber Gloves** – Used for cleaning and medical purposes.

50. **Sunglasses** – Eye protection that became a fashion statement.

51. **Duct Tape** – Versatile adhesive tape.

52. **Peanut Butter** – A popular food invention.

53. **Water Bottles** – Refillable plastic or metal bottles.

54. **Umbrella Hat** – A hat with a small umbrella on top.

55. **Scotch Tape** – Transparent adhesive tape.

56. **Silly Bands** – Shaped rubber bands worn as bracelets.

57. **Wine Corkscrew** – A basic tool for opening wine bottles.

58. **Tic-Tacs** – Small breath freshener mints.

59. **Bic Lighter** – A small disposable lighter.

60. **Hand Warmer Packets** – Small, disposable packets that generate heat.

These simple inventions may appear ordinary, but many have generated millions (or even billions) of dollars due to their widespread use and popularity.

About the Author

In life, Tom is husband to Lucia, father to Jake, brother to John and Peter, a cousin and an uncle, a mentor to a few, a true friend to many, and friendly to everyone.

In business, Tom is a Personal Safety Consultant who has taught in 25 countries, the founder of Invincible: Performance Optimization Coaching, a Motivation Analyst, an engaging speaker, an avid traveler who has visited 40 countries, and an author of fiction and non-fiction books.

You are invited to visit his website
www.TomSotis.com
tom@tomsotis.com

Other books by Tom Sotis

The Way of Tactics

Alexander the Great

History of Greek Warfare

Global Crime Syndicates

Bounty Hunters

Truly Safer

Sharp Strategies

Being a Good Man

The Pursuit of Meaning

Fuel for the Soul

The Echo of Our Soul

Ikigai

Unbreakable Honor

What We Believe

The Character Code

The Art of Character

Timeless Wisdom

Sacred Paths

The Science of Motivation

The Protégé

www.ingramcontent.com/pod-product-compliance
Lightning Source LLC
Chambersburg PA
CBHW060853170526
45158CB00001B/330